Adventures With

Polarfleece®

A Sewing Expedition

Nancy Cornwell

krause publications

700 E. State Street • Iola, WI 54990-0001

krause publications

700 E. State Street • Iola, WI 54990-0001

Krause Publications, Iola, Wisconsin 54990
All rights reserved. First edition printed 1997
Printed in the United States of America

Whenever brand name products are mentioned, it is because I have personally used them and been pleased with the results. In this day and age, with new products being introduced almost daily, there may be other comparable products on the market that will perform the same way. - Nancy Cornwell

The following registered trademark terms and companies appear in this publication:
Polarfleece®, Polartec®, Polartec Power Stretch ®, Polartec Power Dry®, Windbloc®, Element Control™, Moisture Control™ (Malden Mills), Citifleece™, Kinderfleece™, Dyersburg E.C.O.™ Fleece (Dyersburg Corporation), Arctic® Fleece, Chinella™, Chinella Lite™ (Menra Mills), Yukon Fleece™, Nordic Spirit™ (Huntingdon Mills), Solar™ Fleece (Siltex Mills), Berber by Glenoit®, GlenPile®, Zendura®, Glenaura® (Glenoit Mills), Nordic™ Fleece (David Textiles), Kleenex® (Kimberly-Clarke Corporation), Patagonia® (Patagonia Inc.), Woolrich® (Woolrich Inc.), Carter's® (The William Carter Company), Stretch & Sew® (Stretch & Sew Inc.), Kwik Sew® (Kwik Sew Pattern Company), Bernina® (Bernina of America), Lycra™ (DuPont Company), Supplex™ (DuPont), Sulky® Solvy®, Sulky® Sticky™, Totally Stable™ (Gunold + Styckma), Filmoplast Stic™ (Neschen), UltraSuede® (Springs Industries), Polar Piecing™, SnapSetter™ (The Snap Source, Inc.), Stick-It-All™, Cover-Up™, Stick-dSolv™, Fuse 'n Stick™ (Hoop-It-All, Inc.), Fiskar® Diagonal Cutters™ (Fiskars Inc.)

Book Design by Jan Wojtech
Edited by Gabrielle Wyant-Perillo
Illustrations by Digital Graphics, George Maimon
Photography by Ross Hubbard

Cornwell, Nancy.
   Adventures with polarfleece© / Nancy Cornwell.
   p. 160 cm.
   ISBN 0-87341-555-8
   1. Sewing techniques. 2. Sculpturing techniques. 3. Zipper techniques.
   4. Buttonhole Techniques 5. Serger/Sewing techniques. I. Cornwell, Nancy.
   II. Title

                                                                97-74596
                                                                    CIP

Acknowledgments

There may be only one name listed as the author of this book, but there is a huge support team of individuals and companies that deserve a big hug and a heartfelt thanks. The help was given in many ways…physical, factual, mental, emotional and often just plain old "put up with." By the time I finished writing this book, I was referred to as "The Polar Princess" (supposedly it's a compliment, but I'm not so sure…). And so, "The Polar Princess" wishes to acknowledge and thank:

The fantastic group of ladies who make up my store staff. In addition to providing a tremendous amount of inspiration and support, they kept saying "Go home and write. We'll take care of everything here."

Rita Farro, Robbie Fanning, Mary Mulari and Gail Brown who patiently fielded hundreds of questions, all the while encouraging me to "just do it."

A big hug to Rita Farro who actually lost valuable sleep on her personal crusade to come up with the perfect name for this book…and she did, bless her heart.

And to my daughter Jackie Cornwell-McInnes, who added flavor with the "Sewing Expedition" theme.

Joanne Ross, for producing the nationally recognized **Sewing & Stitchery Expo**, the leading consumer sewing show in the country. This tremendous event gave me the opportunity to grow from a store owner… to a speaker… to an author.

Deborah Faupel, Krause Acquisitions Editor, who heard my seminar at the **Sewing & Stitchery Expo** in Puyallup, WA and was bound and determined to "get it in print"… and quickly…

Gabrielle Wyant-Perillo, my editor, who jumped in with both feet and committed to one of the fastest book productions known to mankind. (Gabrielle and the whole Krause Crew belong in the book of records for this one!)

To **Malden Mills**, **Dyersburg Corporation**, **Menra Mills**, **Huntingdon Mills**, **Siltex Mills**, **Glenoit Mills**, and **David Textiles** for their cooperation and information on all their products. It's great companies like these, constantly developing fabulous fabrics that make sewing so much fun.

Sally Dale of **Stroline Textiles** of Seattle and Ann Stables of **Product Solutions** of Seattle for all their helpful background information on fabrications and mills.

Stretch & Sew, Inc. and **Kwik Sew Pattern Company** for providing many of the fleece garments pictured in the book.

To my "I Love To Sew Club™" members, a group of wonderful ladies who love to sew and create. Many of their fleece garments are pictured throughout the book.

My son, Jeff who, in the wisdom of his youth, always managed to lighten things up whenever I took myself too seriously.

My husband, Jeff, who managed the home front and the store front while I researched, typed, experimented, designed, plotted, planned and sewed. I wrote while he ran the business then came home to cook, launder and shop. (That part worked out pretty well and I'm already considering another book!)

And, finally, to all my special customers, both in-store and through mail-order, who make what we do all worthwhile and fun.

To my parents,
Arnold and Evelyn Plein,
who before it was fashionable, instilled in me the belief that I could accomplish anything to which I set my mind and heart.

To my husband,
Jeff, who picked up where my parents left off and for over thirty years has encouraged and supported me in everything I've attempted.

And to my Mother-in-law, Grace Cornwell, without whose tremendous love and support our store would not have become a reality.

Introduction

Polarfleece is the most exciting fabric to hit the sewing industry in fifty years. The colors are bold, the designs outstanding. No longer restricted to outerwear garments, today's designers offer fleece in casual sportswear, pants, tops, sweaters, even dresses and lingerie! It's easy to sew, simple to care for and so scrumptious to wear that it has become the sewing industry's "Most Valuable Player." Polarfleece is a favorite fabric for grandparents, parents, teens and children. Best of all, ready-to-wear garments can be copied at a fraction of the ready-to-wear price!

When Polarfleece, along with all it's relatives, appeared on the market it was love at first touch. Everyone loved wearing it, looking at it, sewing it and playing with it.

One day I was thumbing through a specialty catalog and my eyes fell upon a magnificent polar jacket with glorious tone-on-tone embroidery scrolling down the shawl collar and accenting the cuffs. I was "in love." I wanted it, until I saw the price tag… it was over $300! Common sense won out, but I still coveted that jacket. It intrigued me. I kept mulling "that look" over and over in my mind. It almost became an obsession (sewers are like that). I knew there had to be a way to re-create that look.

Months later, I was in the Garment District, buying ready-to-wear overrun fabrics for my store, and I tripped across a group of embossed fleeces that looked engraved. They were stunning! Instantly my thoughts went back to "that" jacket. The light bulb went on and I figured out how to recreate "that look." The idea for "Sculpturing Polarfleece" was born, and the seeds were planted for writing this book.

Sculpturing Polarfleece is my favorite idea in this whole book. In addition to being fun and easy, it opens up a whole new world of design possibilities. No longer are there just "plain" fleeces, just more fresh canvases on which to work miracles!

Sculpturing offers tremendous creative freedom. It allows you to design your own fabrics! You can create your own coordinating fabrics, change a plain solid fleece into a dramatic plaid, engrave a subtle sports motif on a pullover, add a cute little bunny to an infant's bunting or create a knock-their-socks-off dramatic design on your own "obsession jacket." As you'll find in the "Designer Details" chapter, sculpturing is not only fun and easy, but can be very addictive.

As I started teaching "Sculpturing with Polarfleece" classes, I found that half of the class time was devoted to fielding "how-to" questions. "How do you sew in a zipper and have it lay flat?" "What size needle do I use?" "Do I pretreat?" "What if I can't find ribbing to match?" "Can I use patterns other than fleece patterns?" "How do I make a zippered pocket when my pattern doesn't call for one?" And, most frequently… "How can I get those designer touches found in expensive ready-to-wear clothing?"

Then, at the **Sewing and Stitchery Expo** in Puyallup, Washington, my four scheduled "Playing With Polarfleece" seminars suddenly exploded to nine sold-out seminars. Afterwards, thousands of women said "You talk faster and cover more information than I could possibly take notes on… please write a book!"

And so, I offer you *Adventures With Polarfleece… A Sewing Expedition*.

My intent in writing this book is to share with you those techniques that I have learned over many years of sewing and playing with fleeces, Berbers, plush and pile fabrics. I wanted the flavor of this book to be conversational more like friends talking and sharing information about their favorite hobby, rather than a cut-and-dry instructional approach. I've tossed in many sections labeled as *"Nancy's Hints,"* adding sewing tips that I've found to be especially helpful.

Adventures With Polarfleece will help you to take a commercial pattern and make it your own. There are many excellent commercial and specialty patterns on the market. I personally prefer the variety, fit and ease of sewing offered by **Stretch & Sew** and **Kwik Sew** pattern companies. **Timberlane Press** adds a delightful array of specialty items.

I hope that as you open up a new pattern, you view it as "just a beginning." In this book I offer you a wide variety of techniques, approaches, finishes and alternatives, all found in better ready-to-wear garments. As you expand your sewing horizons, thumb through this book, pick and choose, mix techniques and finishes until you have just the look you want. (You'll probably spend more time "deciding" what to do than actually sewing it! Sewing is the easy part.)

If you are a novice sewer, *Adventures With Polarfleece* will give you the information necessary to confidently explore a whole new world of sewing. If you are a seasoned sewer, you'll find some new avenues to pursue and great ideas with which to play.

Enjoy and have fun!

Love,

Nancy

Foreword

If you are looking for basic information about Polarfleece® – *this is the book*.

If you are interested in how-to sewing techniques and well-written, concise instructions – *this is the book*.

If you already love sewing with Polarfleece and want to learn how to reproduce ready-to-wear designer details – *believe me – THIS IS THE BOOK!*

Nancy Cornwell is a gifted teacher. With everything she does, Nancy brings enthusiasm and a love of sewing. I knew she adored Polarfleece so I figured this book would be good ... really good. But, because of a remarkable collaborative effort between Nancy Cornwell and Krause Publications, this book exceeds even *my* high expectations.

Adventures with Polarfleece breaks new ground in the sewing industry. It is one hundred sixty pages of well-organized, entertaining, action-packed information with over two hundred color photographs! It simply raises the bar...

It starts off by covering the Polarfleece basics. What it is, how to care for it, how to choose patterns, how to alter patterns and how to sew on it. She deals with every question or predicament you could have regarding Polarfleece.

Once you've completed the basic training, the real expedition begins. Nancy is your very capable, well-informed, entertaining tour guide to some exotic new places. Zippers, buttonholes, Lycra trim and accents. During this part of the journey, you will realize how well Nancy understands the complex nature of this exciting new fabric.

And then...just when you think this book has covered every possible aspect of sewing with Polarfleece, Nancy introduces you to some incredible fresh new ideas such as sculpturing.

Sculpturing? Have you ever heard of such a thing?

That's the whole point, don't you see? Nancy uses trims, details and accents, a touch of UltraSuede, an inventive closure, some fresh new sculpturing and turns the otherwise predictable into the truly spectacular.

Nancy Cornwell is to Polarfleece what Admiral Richard Perry was to the North Pole. She is what Steven Spielberg is to movies and what Oprah Winfrey is to talk shows. Nancy covers new turf. She's a pioneer – and has boldly gone where no person has gone before. And, she does it like a true explorer, with breathtaking exuberance.

So buckle up – you're in for quite a ride!

Rita Farro
Author of *Life is Not a Dress Size*

TABLE OF CONTENTS

Introduction ix

PART ONE   14

WHAT'S IN A NAME

Polarfleece and Polartec - Malden Mills, U.S.A
Citifleece, Kinderfleece and E.C.O. Fleece -
    Dyersburg Corporation, U.S.A.
Arctic, Chinella and Chinella Lite - Menra Mills,
    U.S.A.
Yukon Fleece and Nordic Spirit - Huntingdon Mills,
    Canada
Solar Fleece - Siltex Mills, Canada
Berber by Glenoit; Zendura, Glenarua - Glenoit Mills,
    U.S.A.
"Offshore" Fleeces - Taiwan and the Orient
Nordic Fleece - David Textiles, U.S.A.
Fleece Fabrics and Pile Fabrics - What's The
    Difference
How Do I Use This Information?

PART TWO   24

BASICS YOU NEED TO KNOW

Determining The Right and Wrong Side
    Cutting Out Fleece
Fabric and Garment Care; Pre-treating, Laundering,
    Pressing
Sewing Machine Basics; Thread, Needles, Stitch
    Length, Machine Care
Serger Basics; Stitch Choice, Cutting Width,
    Differential Feed, Machine Care
"Gotta-Have" Notions
A Word About Adhesives
Troubleshooting - Quick Reference Guide

PART THREE   36

PATTERN CHOICES AND DESIGN CHANGES

Pattern Choices; Things to Consider When Using
Patterns Not Designed For Fleece, Sleeve Cap,
Sizing, Simple Design Changes; Color-Blocking,
Copy-Cat Designer Collar, No-Fail Collar Change,
Eliminating Separate Elastic Casings, No Side-Seam
Jackets and Vests

PART FOUR   46

SEAM OPTIONS

Traditional 5/8"
Traditional 1/4"
Lapped Seams
Blunt-Edged Patch Pockets
Blunt-Edged Collars

PART FIVE   52

READY-TO-WEAR EDGE FINISH TECHNIQUES

A Word About Using Nylon Lycra Trim
Wrapped Edge Finishes
    Lycra Wrapped Edges - The "Real" Way (The Hard
        Way)
    Lycra Wrapped Edges - The "Cheater's" Way (The
        Easy Way)
    Ribbing Wrapped Edges
    Ribbing Wrap With Elastic (Ribbing That Acts
        Like Lycra!)
    Self-Fabric Wrapped Edges - a.k.a. Fat Piping
Wimpy Ribbing Dilemma and Solutions
Self-Fabric Trim
Backward Topstitching
Elastic Cuffs and Hems

PART SIX   68

NO-HASSLE ZIPPERS

No-Bulk Zipper Shortening
Traditional Zipper Application with Tips
Untraditional Method - Blunt Edge Method
Traditional Without Facing - Naked Zipper
Patagonia Wrap - Or, How To Dress The Naked
    Zipper
Wrapped Edge Zipper Insertion
Super Easy Zippered Pockets
Cut and Sew Pocket
Two-From-One Zipper Trick
"Backwards" Zipper
  Color Options
  Zipper Application
  Neck Seam Finish
  Neckline Guidelines
      Regular Collar or Baseball Style Ribbing
      Zipper Through the Collar Style
      Finished Neck Edge with Hood
Coordinating "Backwards Patch Pockets"
Coordinating "Backwards Roll-up Cuffs"

PART SEVEN   84

BUTTONHOLES ON FLEECE - CHALLENGES AND SOLUTIONS

Golden Rule of Buttonholes
Challenge #1 and Solutions
Challenge #2 and Solutions
Challenge #3 and Solutions
Challenge #4 and Solutions
Too Good To Be True Buttonhole
Sport Snaps

PART EIGHT   90

A TOUCH OF CLASS - ULTRASUEDE ACCENTS

Drawcord or Hood Tie
Buttonhole Loops
Buttonhole Tabs
Buttonhole Patches
Buttonhole Patches with Loops
Pockets
Zipper Pulls
Zipper Tab
Pocket Flaps
Yokes
Piping

PART NINE   98

DESIGNER DETAILS

Sculpturing Polarfleece
  Planning Directions
  Design Choices
  Meandering
  Checks and Plaids
  Outline Sculpturing - Quilted Look
  Single Motif
  Over-Sized Designs
Polar Pintucks
Best of Both Worlds - Sculpturing and Pintucks!
Embroidery on Fleece
Appliqué on Fleece

PART TEN   110

THE GALLERY

PART ELEVEN   131

PLAYING WITH POLARFLEECE

Jacket With Dramatic Sculptured Back
Diamond Lattice Appliqué
Make It Your Way No Side Seam Vest
Elegant and Easy Polar Cape
Patchwork Pullover
Snuggle Bag
"No-Brainer" Blanket
Naptime Buddy - made to "fit"
Little Lady's Polar Wardrobe; Kilt, Vest, 5-Minute
    Hat, Scarf
Baby Collection; Blanket, Pillow, Appliqué and Toy
Baby Snuggle Wrap

HAPPY ENDINGS - WHAT TO DO WITH THE LEFTOVERS

5-Minute Hat
6-Minute Hat
Simple Scarf or Muffler
Mittens for Kids
Flower Pin

ABOUT THE AUTHOR

PART ONE
WHAT'S IN A NAME?

In this day and age of mass marketing campaigns and huge advertising budgets, we are very "brand name" conscious. In reference to food, computers, clothing or fabrics, brand names provide a known quality, credibility and accountability.

When customers come into our store requesting "Polarfleece," they are asking for a high quality, double-sided, napped polyester fleece. They use the word "polarfleece" as though it was a "type" of fabric rather than a "brand name" of fabric.

For instance, the name "Kleenex™" solely belongs to Kimberly-Clarke®, and refers to a specific brand product. Yet, "kleenex" has became a household word meaning "tissue." Although there is a wide range of "tissues" on the market, from high quality name brands to inferior quality discount tissues, everyone calls them "kleenex," as though that were a generic word for the product. The same applies to the word "Polarfleece."

The name Polarfleece is a trademark word which belongs to Malden Mills. As often happens when any great product comes on the market, other companies "jump on the bandwagon" and create similar products.

The mills discussed below are the major players in today's market. Known for high quality, they are the leaders in the apparel field. The fabrics created by these mills are most frequently found in better name brand apparel and are now available to the home sewer.

POLARFLEECE & POLARTEC from Malden Mills, U.S.A.

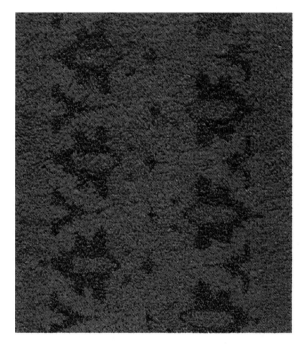

In 1979, when Malden Mills first sold their fleece to Patagonia, the word "Polarfleece" quickly became a household word. Everyone wanted a Polarfleece Patagonia jacket. The fleece is revolutionary in that it is lightweight, yet warm.

The fabric is also hydrophobic, meaning that it "hates water." Polarfleece picks up less than 1% of its weight in moisture. Even when soaking wet, the fabric continues to maintain loft and insulating characteristics. Polarfleece is perfect outerwear fabric as it actively wicks moisture away from the body.

Malden's Research and Development department improved Polarfleece (creating a non-pill finish) and developed a specialized product line called Polartec. The Polarfleece line is geared toward the fashion market while the Polartec line is geared toward the outdoor enthusiast who faces many different climate conditions. The fleeces can be worn alone or layered for serious climate control.

The Polartec fleece line includes a variety of fleece types and frequently refers to a 100, 200 or 300 weight series. These numbers signify lightweight (5.5 to 11 ounces per linear yard), medium weight (12 to 16 ounces per linear yard) and heavier weight fleeces (16.5 to 20 ounces per linear yard). *Note: The ounce weights are approximate and ever-changing.*

The major function of the 100 weight fleece is moisture control. The 100 weight wicks perspiration away from the body to keep the skin dry and is typically worn closest to the body. Polartec 100 series, Power Stretch, Power Dry and the Micro Series are part of Malden's moisture control family and have an anti-microbial finish to prevent odor causing bacteria. They are used in shirts, pants, underwear and accessories.

The major function of the 200 and 300 weight fleece is temperature control. These weights provide warmth, they breathe to allow body vapor to escape from the inner layers, they are worn layered and frequently have a water repellent finish. Polartec 200 and 300 Series and Series Bipolar belong to these categories and are used in jackets, pullovers, pants, and accessories.

Malden continually conducts intensive research and testing programs to develop exceptional fabrics that will perform well in specific conditions. Windbloc and Thermal Stretch are Polartec fabrics designed for element control and are used in outerwear garments.

Polarfleece and Polartec are the fleece names most recognized by the home sewer. They are featured in Patagonia, L.L. Bean, Woolrich, Timberland, Columbia Sportswear, Marmot Mountain Works, Lands' End and REI private label garments.

CITIFLEECE, KINDERFLEECE & E.C.O. FLEECE from Dyersburg Corporation, U.S.A.

Dyersburg Fabrics started as a family-owned business in 1929. Primarily known as the makers of cotton sweaters, long johns and cotton fleece gloves, they are responsible for some very important "firsts."

In the 1930's Dyersburg introduced the first knitted fleece fabric which was a wool blend for women's coats. They expanded and began producing blanket sleepers with this fabric.

In 1972 the company introduced the first flame retardant fleece.

Twenty years later, they introduced

E.C.O. Fleece, the first post-consumer recycled fleece fabricated from plastic soda pop bottles.

Citifleece is a polyester fleece engineered for the sportswear market. It can be found in many private labels and high quality ready-to-wear brands such as Chaps by Ralph Lauren.

Kinderfleece is a soft and cuddly fleece engineered for the children's playwear market. This fabric is found in garments by Oshkosh B' Gosh, Healthtex, Buster Brown, William Carter, J.C. Penney private label as well as additional private labels.

ARCTIC, CHINELLA & CHINELLA LITE
from Menra Mills, U.S.A.

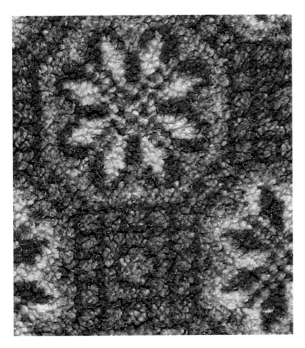

For over fifteen years, Menra Mills has been a leading fleece manufacturer for major and private label apparel manufacturers in the outdoor and activewear market. Menra is known for unique surface textures, special finishes, microfibers and technical laminates. The fleeces they manufacture are primarily 100%

polyester and used in mid-layer and outer-layer skiwear, outerwear, sweaters and accessories.

Menra does not heavily promote their "trademarked names." A variety of Menra fleece types are used by Eddie Bauer, L.L. Bean, and many private labels.

YUKON FLEECE & NORDIC SPIRIT
from Huntingdon Mills, Canada

The Yukon Fleece series is the trademarked name of Huntingdon Mills of Canada, another extensive producer of high quality fleece. They offer Yukon Fleece Lights (lightweight), Yukon Fleece 2000 (mid-weight), Yukon Fleece (mid to heavyweight), as well as Yukon Fleece Protec fabrics which are laminated with a waterproof and windproof breathable membrane. These are designed to protect against demanding situations. Nordic Spirit is an elegant line of plush pile fabrics featured in high fashion clothing lines. Huntingdon Mills fabrics are used by Columbia Sportswear, Nordstrom private label and numerous specialty private labels.

SOLAR FLEECE from Siltex Mills, Canada

Siltex Mills is known for high quality cotton knit lines as well as a beefy 17 1/2 ounce Solar Fleece line. Solar Fleece is used by many manufacturers who produce licensed NFL and NHL goods and private label companies in U.S.A., Canada, Asia, and Europe.

Siltex primarily develops products for small manufacturers and retail. Their research and development department works closely with yarn suppliers and finishers to continually improve and develop products to meet specific customer requirements. Many significant name brand manufacturers are using Solar Fleece in their lines, as is apparent by the Solar Fleece hang tag on ready-to-wear garments.

To determine the **right** and **wrong** side of Solar Fleece, study the cut edge and determine the "thick" side and the "thin"

side. Siltex shears one side to reduce pilling, causing one side to be thinner. The "thin" side is the **right** side of the fabric and is to be worn facing out.

BERBER by Glenoit, ZENDURA, GLENAURA, from Glenoit Mills, U.S.A.

Glenoit is a privately owned company which was founded over fifty years ago. The largest manufacturer of pile fabrics in North America, Glenoit is known world-wide for high quality. They produce pile fabrics on computerized sliver knitting machines and have brought a sense of fashion to the outdoor and sportswear apparel market.

GlenPile is the name given to the high-tech category of pile fabrics specifically engineered for outdoor and active apparel.

Berber by Glenoit is distinguished by its heather-flecked, softly curled surface which is made from a combination of fibers.

Zendura is identifiable by its thick, lush, curled Sherpa appearance. Glenaura has a plush texture similar to velvet. Zendura and Glenaura are very dramatic and frequently combined in a hi-low jacquard pattern for high-fashion designs.

GlenPile is most noted for its very soft hand and drape-able nature. Glenoit pile fabrics are featured in Nautica, Tommy Hilfiger, Polo by Ralph Lauren, Liz Claiborne, Sierra Designs, Marmot Mountain Works, LL Bean, plus private labels for Nordstrom and REI.

NC's Note of Interest: Malden, Dyersburg, Huntingdon and Glenoit Mills are vertical mills.

"Vertical" means the companies are in complete control of every step and stage of production. Production includes dyeing, carding, blending, knitting and finishing. Because of such involvement in production the quality control is exceptional.

"OFFSHORE" FLEECES imported from Taiwan and the Orient

When you buy a washing machine with a Sears name on it, that machine isn't made by Sears. It is made by a major appliance manufacturer *for* Sears to meet their specifications. Similarly, offshore mills manufacture a wide variety of fleeces for American companies. They are individually contracted to make fleece in specific qualities. The degrees of quality vary.

There is an advantage of sewing with a highly recognized brand name in that you are dealing with a "known" entity that has a history and a proven track record. Price however, is an advantage of sewing with "offshore" goods. The prices vary as much as the quality. The two tend to be in direct proportion to each other. See the section entitled "So How Do I Use This Information?" for assistance in quality identification.

Note: "You get what you pay for."

NORDIC FLEECE from David Textiles, U.S.A.

My favorite offshore fleece is manufactured for and imported by David Textiles.

It carries the trademarked name "Nordic" fleece and is a consistent high quality, high loft, mid-weight polyester fleece. The new heathered fleeces are a polyester and rayon blend.

David Textiles is one of the few converters who supply the home sewing market as well as many private label companies.

Noteworthy: Nordic fleece passed U.S. and Japanese testing with the highest ratings. Nordic Fleece is heavily used in baby and children's wear as it tests formaldehyde-free.

FLEECE FABRICS & PILE FABRICS
WHAT'S THE DIFFERENCE?

In general, for the purposes of this book, the word "fleece" is used to encompass all polar-type fleece and pile fabrics. In terms of sewing techniques, care and handling, appropriate pattern choices and design choices, the same principles apply to both fabric categories, unless otherwise stated.

Today's fleece and pile fabrics are high-tech, high performance products that are very easy to sew because they are extremely forgiving. Both types are equally warm and soft to the touch. Both wick moisture away from the body, so that they feel dry, even when soaking wet. Both offer tremendous warmth in comparison to their weight and offer high fashion colors, textures and designs. Nevertheless there are many differences. Study the following lists to determine which fleece fabric will best meet your needs.

Construction

Fleece fabrics are made by first twisting fibers into yarns. The yarns are then knitted into fabric. To raise fibers and create a downy surface, the fabric is brushed with wire brushes. This process makes the cloth compact. Finally, the fleece is then sheared and finished.

Pile fabrics are slightly lighter in weight and, rather than being first twisted into yarns, are created directly from fiber into fabric. The loose fibers are dyed, mixed, and combed into a long, soft, fluffy "rope". This "rope" is then guided into a sliver knitting machine which permanently locks the fibers onto a fine denier backing. The pile is the result of the individual "hairs" standing on end. It is then sheared and finished.

Fiber Content

Fleece is predominantly made from 100% polyester. However, it can be blended with other materials such as Lycra, cotton, wool and rayon.

Pile fabrics are generally made from acrylic or microfiber acrylic and blended with some polyester. Similar to fleece, pile fabrics can be made from any mixture of man-made and natural fibers. Acrylics are the fiber of choice because they mimic natural fibers. They can be easily curled and crimped for more warmth and textured for interesting surface effects.

Warmth Per Weight

Fleece is first spun into a yarn which adds weight. It is then brushed to compact the fabric and to build in air pockets for insulation. Pile offers more warmth per weight by nature of its construction. The insulation qualities are derived from the natural ability of the fiber to trap air pockets. Since the fiber in pile fabrics is not spun, the technical qualities of the fibers are not altered.

Microfiber acrylics offer even more air pockets.

As a result of this process, pile offers more warmth per weight. Fleece offers more wind resistance per weight. High quality fabrics provide more warmth.

Wicking

Wicking, also referred to as moisture management, is equivalent to capillary action in material. The fabric is constructed in such a way to allow the moisture to travel along the fibers or yarns and away from the body. Some lighter weight fleeces have an added chemical application to promote wicking of moisture away from the body. This chemical application is found only on the lighter weight fleeces because they are worn next to the body.

Water Repellency

Polyester and acrylic fibers are hydro-phobic by nature. This means that they "hate" and retain little water. With the technology of microfibers (fine denier yarns), these fabrics repel water by construction. Durable Water Repellent or DWR, a semi-permanent substance, is applied to the surface of some mid-weight and heavy weight fleeces to further repel moisture.

Breathability

Fleece and pile fabric rate very closely. Pile fabrics were not compacted with the "brushing" stage that fleece goes through to be napped and therefore have a slightly higher rating.

Color & Design

Fleece fabrics are dyed or surface printed after the knitting process. Most printed fleeces are 200 or mid-weight.

Pile fabrics are made on high tech Jacquard machines that are programmed to produce intricate prints and color combinations.

Drape & Feel

Both fabrications offer a wide range of weights and finishes. Generally speaking, fleeces are firm and have a little more bulk, while pile fabrics are soft and drape better. Originally, fleeces were totally geared toward outerwear apparel, while pile fabrics were aimed at fashion garments. With the introduction of microfibers, computer technology in the knitting industry and the variety of finishes and weights, both fabric types now crossover between weather-beater and fashion apparel.

Pilling

Many of today's fleeces claim "no pilling." However, a more accurate claim would be "low pilling."

Pilling is the formation of little balls of fiber on the surface of the fabric. These balls result from contact, abrasion and wear. As fabric rubs against fabric, fiber is pulled away from the yarn and raises to the surface of the fabric. This occurs in all fabrics and cannot be avoided. Pills are not as noticeable on natural fabrics because the fibers are not as strong as synthetic fibers. When pills rise to the surface on natural fabrics, they break and fall off.

Manmade fibers such as polyester and acrylic, which constitute most fleece and pile fabrics, are very strong. When the fiber pills on the surface of these fabrics, the manmade fiber is so strong that it won't release the pill. Therefore, the pill remains stuck on the fabric. Again, all fabrics pill, but it is most noticeable on the fabrics made from stronger, manmade fibers.

The fleeces of yesteryear were notorious for pilling. Hanging on the rack in the stores, the garments looked as though they had been through World War III! Today's technology has assisted in the production of many very low pill fabrics. With the introduction of microfibers and the newer finishing techniques, high quality fleece and pile fabrics now have low-pill finishes that look excellent after wearing and laundering.

Note: Pilling is more prevalent in lower quality fleeces because less money was invested in quality fibers and finishing processes. Many times inferior quality isn't apparent until after wearing and laundering.

Upkeep

I found a clever little trick to "freshen up" fleece garments. The little brush on the end of your travel steamer is perfect for "brushing" fleece. Don't use the steam... just the brush!

End Use

New high-tech fabrics are being introduced almost daily. Both fleece and pile fabrics offer a wide range of weights, finishes, features and fabrications. In general, fleece fabrics offer more hard-use, weather-beater options while pile fabrics offer more options in fashionable sportswear.

Finishes

The surface appearance of the fleece or pile fabric is a direct result of shearing and finishing techniques. Shearing is a finishing process done by a machine that is similar to a lawn mower. Shearing controls the length of the pile or nap and, depending upon the techniques used, may create a patterned or smooth surface. A sculptured effect is achieved by flattening portions of the pile with an engraved roller and shearing the remaining erect areas.

Berber has a softly curled, nubby surface that is distinguished by a flecked appearance, resulting from a combination of fibers. It generally has a soft sweater-knit backing.

Shearling and **Sherpa** have a lamb's wool appearance that is achieved by curling the pile or surface nap.

Plush has a velvet-like appearance resulting from dense fibers that are evenly sheared.

Faux Fur is a pile fabric with deep pile that simulates the fur of animals. Because of its construction and long pile, faux fur techniques are different than the fleece and pile techniques discussed in this book.

Fleece or Pile? Pile or Fleece?

One is not better than the other. Choose the weight and characteristics to compliment the garment you are creating.

SO, YOU ARE ASKING... "HOW DO I USE THIS INFORMATION?"

When a trademarked name is on a ready-to-wear garment, it gives information identifying who made the fabric and a certain level of quality. The same holds true to labeled fleece yardage.

Be aware however, in today's sewing

market, that it is not always easy to know exactly what you are purchasing.

When fabric stores buy directly from a mill representative or from a major distributor, the bolt end labels carry the trademarked name and fabric contents.

A good portion of the sportswear fleeces are purchased from jobbers. Jobbers are companies who buy first quality overages directly from the mills, mill "seconds" (which they clean up and resell) and manufacturer's overruns.

When fabric stores purchase overruns, "cleaned up" seconds, or flat folds, the trademarked name is not usually provided.

Here is where the discriminating sewer must put her skills to work to determine the quality of a particular fabric. Ask yourself the following questions:

Is it thick and lofty?

Is it dense?

Can I see threads under the nap or is it plush?

If I rub it against itself does it pill easily?

Is the print clear?

Is the design printed relatively straight on grain?

Does the stretch have nice recovery or is it lax?

Does it "feel" good?

Is the price too good to be true?

Again, "you get what you pay for."

High quality fleeces are made from superior yarns, are knitted thicker and more dense and are brushed to raise the nap.

Next they are "veloured." Velouring is a process which results in a fine raised finish. Lower quality fleece manufacturers use cheaper yarns, knit less densely and disregard the velouring process. This accounts for the excessive pilling of lower quality fleeces.

Finally the fabric is sheared to reduce pilling.

Fortunately, for the first time in quite awhile, sewers have the opportunity to be creative and save money. Fleece garments can be made at well under half the cost of purchased ready-to-wear garments. Before investing time, money and effort, make sure you are buying fleece and pile fabric of a suitable quality.

Note: A Fact of Life: There are times when a "to-die-for" print is found on a low quality fabric. Sometimes you just "gotta have it." If you love it, buy it. But, don't invest a lot of time and effort creating a masterpiece because it will have a very short life span.

REMINDER:

For the purposes of this book, the term "fleece" applies to all brands; Polarfleece, Polartec, Yukon Fleece, Arctic Fleece, Nordic Fleece, GlenPile, Berbers, sherpas, shearlings, plush fabrics, and so on. Notations will be made if and when there are specific differences.

PART TWO

BASICS YOU NEED TO KNOW

DETERMINING THE RIGHT AND WRONG SIDE OF FLEECE

One of the most frequently asked questions is "How can I tell which is the right side of the fabric?"

It is important to know which is the right side (the face), because that is the side that will wear better, and look nicer, for a longer length of time. If a water repellent was applied, it was done so to the face of the fabric and should be worn facing the weather.

When working with fleece, it is often not obvious which is the right side. There are many "oldtime" little sewer's tricks and rules that don't necessarily pertain to the fleece category. Perhaps you think that fabrics are always bolted "face out." This is not necessarily true.

Realize, when purchasing fleece from a favorite fabric store, that the fabric comes into the store in a variety of ways and that there are several variables in fabric presentation.

First, fleece may have been purchased doubled and rolled, on the bolt, right side out or wrong side out. The store buyer dictates how the fabric, rolled onto the bolt core, will arrive. This is often dependent upon whether the store displays the fabric draped or laying flat.

Perhaps the fabric was purchased on a large roll and the store staff did the actual bolting.

Or, the fabrics may come in flat folds of short cuts, usually less than five yards. The flat fold can be displayed on a table or rolled onto bolt cores.

Another possibility is that the fabrics were purchased as poundage goods and tossed into a huge box. The store personnel sorted, folded and put the fabric pieces in order for sale.

It is impossible to apply any hard and fast rules for determining which is the right and wrong side according to how the fabric is wrapped on the bolt or how it is lying on a display table.

At this point, determining which is the right and wrong side of the fabric falls onto the sewer's shoulders. Following are tips to ease the process of determination: On textured, plush, Berber and pile fabrics, there is a definite and obvious, right and wrong side so there should be no problem making that decision.

On printed fleeces you will frequently find the design is more crisp, clean and attractive on one side. The appearance of the fabric determines which is the **right** side.

A wide range of double-sided fleeces appear to be the same on both sides. This can be frustrating for the discriminating sewer who has a burning desire to know which side the manufacturer considers the "right side."

On a quest to have this question answered, I called six manufacturers and asked, "How do I determine the right side of your fabric?" They all said, "Most of the time (but not always), when you pull along the selvage edges, the fabric will curl to the **right** side (that's tugging on the lengthwise grain). If you pull on the crossgrain it will curl to the **wrong** side."

The "most of the time" portion of the above statement unnerved me, so I developed additional criteria for determining the right and wrong side.

> ## NANCY'S HINT:
>
> In order of importance. If the first guideline doesn't give you a definitive decision, go onto the next guideline.

"LOOKS"

Choose the best looking side. Obviously if one side looks more attractive, that's the side that should face out. If the selvage also curls to the attractive side, than the right side has been positively identified.

WATER REPELLENCY TEST

Pour water on both sides of the fabric and take notice whether the water beads up more on one side. Some fleeces are treated with a water repellent finish. If this is the case, wear the water repellent side face out.

"ROUGH IT UP"

After use, the right and the wrong side will usually wear differently. The right side will pill less and look better. To discern how both sides react, "rough them up" by rubbing the fabric aggressively against itself. Do this on both sides and examine which is a little "worse for wear." This will be the wrong side.

CUT EDGE EXAMINATION

Examine the cut edge of the fleece. If a definite thicker side and thinner side can be determined, choose the thinner side as the face.

Double-sided fleeces are made with the same thickness on both sides. They are then sheared for reduced pilling. If only one side was sheared, the thinner side will be the "less pill" side. *Note: This does not hold true if one side was fashion textured.*

If the above tests have been performed and you are still unable to discern a difference, just choose a side and deem it "the right side!"

NC's Exception: Let's say I have just chosen four delicious solid colors of fleece from the mountain of flat folds in the fabric store. My plan is to make a dynamic color-blocked top. I have gone through the guidelines above and still haven't determined an obvious right and wrong side. I know that after wearing and laundering, my right and wrong sides will react differently from each other. In this instance I would pre-treat my fleeces before sewing.

I have noted later in this chapter that it is not necessary to pre-treat fleeces for shrinkage or color bleeding. However, in this instance I would pre-treat the fleeces, so that I can compare both sides of each fabric and choose which looks best before I start sewing. I can then be assured of choosing consistently and having a great looking color-blocked top after numerous wearings and washings!

CUTTING OUT FLEECE

Lay out all pattern pieces using the "with nap" layout.

There are two schools of thought regarding nap. One teaches "rough down" for richer color and is more noticeable on darker colors. The other teaches "smooth down" for comfortable wearing and results in a lighter, more frosted color appearance.

Stand in front of a mirror and hold up the fabric both ways. Stroke the fleece from shoulder towards the floor and determine a "rough" and a "smooth" direction. Choose the most pleasing direction.

Note: I suggest using the smooth down on longer pile fabrics, plush fabrics and faux furs.

Some fleeces have distinct naps, while others have no discernible differences. Even if the difference is not noticable, choose one direction and lay out all of the pattern pieces in the same direction. This eliminates potential surprises. When you are walking down the street, you sure don't want one sleeve to look different from the rest of the garment!

After the right side of the fabric and the direction of the nap has been determined, it is important to be absolutely religious and meticulously consistent when laying out the pattern pieces and cutting out the fabric. Establish and follow a routine...and stick to it!

A LITTLE PREVENTATIVE MEDICINE BY "DR." NANCY

To avoid errors, establish a routine when cutting out fleece fabrics.

Always mark the **wrong** side of the fabric on **all** cutout garment pieces. Use a good chalk marker that doesn't easily rub off. I prefer Clover™ Chacopel Pencils because they mark easily and stay put until I rub the marks away. In addition, if I mark on the wrong side of the fabric, I don't even have to bother rubbing the marks away! They are on the wrong side and will never show!

It is also acceptable to mark with safety pins.

On the **wrong** side of the cutout garment pieces, mark center fronts with a single hash mark and center backs with a double hash mark. Also mark, as necessary, important notches and dots on sleeves, facings and other pertinent pattern pieces. The purpose of this is to avoid confusion when you get to the sewing machine.

On such pieces as collars, cuffs, patch pockets and pieces that are uniform in shape, mark the "**top edge**" on the **wrong** side. This assures that the pieces will be sewn together correctly, with the naps running consistently.

Mark notches with a fabric pencil instead of clipping. Clipped notches will weaken a 1/4" seam.

Follow a simple routine, all the time, every time, and you will find there is less room for error. Also, if the project is put on the back burner for two months, when "tackling" it again, you will know exactly what the markings mean and allow you to proceed with confidence.

FABRIC & GARMENT CARE

PRETREATMENT

I know, the "golden rule" states "always pre-treat fabrics before cutting them out," however, I "cheat" when working with fleeces. Fleeces don't shrink unless overdried in a hot dryer and the colors don't run. So, there is really no need for pre-treatment.

The only time I pre-treat my fleece is when I have difficulty determining the right and wrong sides of the fabric. (See "Exception" in Nancy's Guidelines for Determining Right & Wrong Side.)

LAUNDERING

To avoid unnecessary abrasion, wash separately or with similar garments. Launder garments inside out.

Use a powdered detergent and launder in a luke-warm wash on gentle cycle.

Note: Liquid detergents can alter the effectiveness of the moisture wicking chemical treatment on some lighter weight fleeces.

Do not use bleach, fabric softeners or water softeners.

Note: Softeners have an adverse effect on the Durable Water Repellent (DWR) chemical finish that is applied to the surface of some mid-weight and heavy weight fleeces.

Tumble dry on a low setting, short cycle to restore the downy appearance. Note: Since fleeces are hydrophobic, they repel water and dry quickly. Over-drying or the use of high heat will cause unnecessary shrinkage and will shorten the life-span of the garment. Easiest way to dry? Shake and hang to dry.

Dry cleaning is not recommended.

PRESSING

Pressing is not necessary nor recommended.

If, during the construction stages, pressing seems necessary, hold the iron above the fabric and steam. Gently finger press to "encourage" the fleece to set in the desired position. Never place an iron directly onto the fabric. Direct contact may leave a permanent imprint or melt the fabric.

SEWING MACHINE BASICS

Make sure the sewing machine you are about to use is cleaned, oiled and in good working order.

THREAD

Choose a good quality, long staple, polyester thread to match your fabric, or a shade darker.

Note: Don't waste your time with bargain five for $1 threads. They will knot, fray, break and cause nothing but frustration.

NEEDLES

Always begin a project with a fresh, new needle.

Because fleeces are knitted fabrics, choose a Universal, Stretch or Ballpoint needle.

Note: These needles have rounded points that deflect the yarns rather than pierce them.

Choose the needle size according to the weight of the fleece. Recommended sizes for light fleeces: 70/10 or 75/11 Stretch; mid-weight 80/12 or 90/14; heavy weight 100/16. Use the smallest size needle possible that is strong enough for the job.

But...and there's always a "but"...

The more you experiment with fleece and pile fabrics and the more you explore different design details, additional elements need to be considered when choosing needles.

As the components of a sewing project change, the needle choices will also change. The needle choice is dictated by the "fussiest" or most temperamental element of the project.

For Example

If UltraSuede detailing is added and the Universal needle's stitching is not acceptable, change to a Stretch 11 or Stretch 14 needle.

Note: UltraSuede is "fussier" than fleece and sews better with a Stretch needle.

If top-stitching on UltraSuede with metallic thread, change to an Embroidery or Metallic needle.

Note: Sewing with metallic thread is more temperamental than sewing on UltraSuede or fleece and sews better with the larger eye of this specialty needle.

Choose a Stretch needle if sewing on Lycra fleece.

Note: Lycra sews better with Stretch needles.

STITCH LENGTH

Use the fewest number of stitches per inch while maintaining garment functionality. As a rule, this is 7 to 9 stitches per inch or a 3mm to 3.5mm stitch length. This length is appropriate for most loose fitting fleece garments with no high stress seams.

Note: A stitch length that is too short tends to stretch fleece.

In closer fitting garments that require the seams to "give," shorten the stitch length to 12 to 14 stitches per inch or a 2mm to 2.5 mm stitch length.

SERGER BASICS

SAME AS THE SEWING MACHINE BASICS, WITH THE ADDITION OF...

STITCH CHOICE

Use a three/four thread serger seam. If working with a three-thread serger, supplement the serger seam with a straight-stitch from a conventional sewing machine.

CUTTING WIDTH

If your serger allows you to change the cutting width by moving the cutting blade, narrow the cutting width to cut off more fabric and relieve "jam-packing" the heavier fleece in the narrow seam allowance.

DIFFERENTIAL FEED

For seams to lay flat on fleeces with more stretch, adjust differential as necessary to 1 or 1.5.

MACHINE & SERGER UPKEEP

Sewing with fleece and pile fabrics causes great amounts of lint to accumulate inside the machines. A lot of lint build-up is found under the needle plate and at the top of the needle bar. Because lint soaks up the machine oil, it is important to frequently dismantle and thoroughly clean the machine. Oil the machines according to the owners manual instructions.

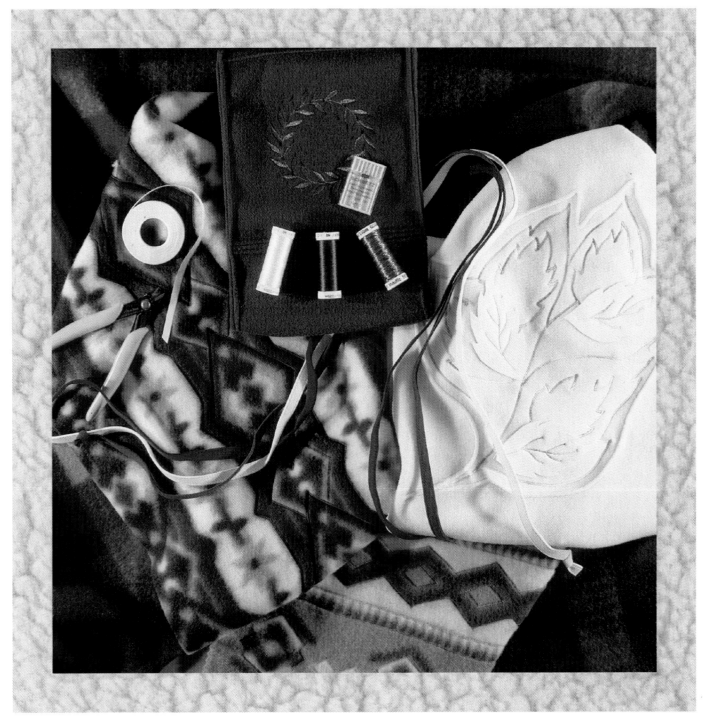

Note: I mention the following products throughout the book because I have used them and have been pleased with their performance. There may be similar products available that will also work.

WASH–A–WAY WONDERTAPE, 1/4" DOUBLE-SIDED BASTING TAPE BY COLLINS

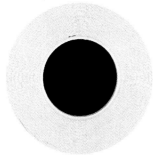

In my opinion, this is the only way to "baste" zippers and pockets.
• Perfect for holding garment pieces in place where pins would be awkward.
• No need to remove, it dissolves in the laundry.
• Does not gum up the needle.
• You will soon discover how terrific this tape is and find yourself taping yards and yards of trim, and then stitching in place. This product will not typically gum up the needle. However, with excessive use you may occassionally experience a sticky needle. To remove buildup, simply wipe the needle with rubbing alcohol.

LONG GLASS HEAD PINS

Since pins can be easily lost in the loft of the fabric, choose longer pins. Pin at a 90° angle to the seamline or cut edges.

CHACOPEL PENCILS

Chacopel pencils are fabric marking pencils from Clover. These are my favorite fabric pencils because they mark easily on fleece and stay marked until I "rub it out."

FISKAR DIAGONAL CUTTERS

The perfect tool to shorten plastic-toothed sport zippers.

SOLVY

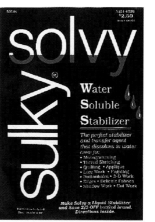

Solvy is a water-soluble stabilizer by Sulky. It is perfect for creating good-looking buttonholes and is also used for machine embroidery.

STICK–DSOLV

Stick-dSolv is an adhesive backed water-soluble stabilizer from Hoop-It-All, Inc. It is an adhesive stabilizer with wash-away features. This product does not leave a residue. Use for buttonholes and embroidery.

COVER-UP

Cover-Up is a permanent stabilizer from Hoop-It-All, Inc. and is used to prevent color "show-through" on machine embroidery.

FUSE 'N STICK

Another Hoop-It-All, Inc. product, this tacky adhesive allows you to position and adhere an appliqué onto fleece before stitching. Fuse it to the applique, stick in onto the fleece.

STICKY BACK (BY SULKY), STICK-IT-ALL LIGHT (BY HOOP-IT-ALL, INC.) OR FILMOPLAST STIC

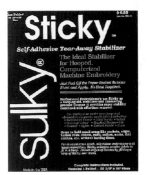

These are adhesive-backed papers used with embroidery machines. Hoop the paper instead of the fabric and adhere the fabric to the adhesive paper!

TOTALLY STABLE

Totally Stable is a temporary press-on tear away stabilizer from Sulky. It is used on fleeces for sculpture stitching.

LONG-PRONGED SPORT SNAPS & SNAPSETTER

These snaps and setting tool, from The Snap Source, are the perfect alternative to buttons and buttonholes.

LARGE (60MM) ROTARY CUTTER

Rotary cutters are available from numerous companies. Bulky fleeces are much easier to

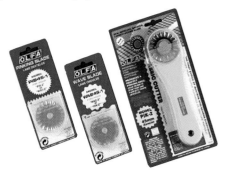

cut with the larger blade and handle. However, you'll find that they are wonderful for all your cutting needs!

A WORD ABOUT ADHESIVES

The following information applies to all arenas of sewing. Learn the principles of adhesives and you will avoid hassle when it is time to remove them.

TACKY ADHESIVES

The chemical make-up and design of a tacky adhesive causes a stronger hold the longer it is in place. Imagine cellophane tape placed on a window. If peeled off in one minute, it comes off quite easily. However, if you wait a day or two the job is not so easy. The same principle applies to tacky adhesives used in sewing.

TEAR-AWAY STABILIZERS, FILMS, TAPES

The longer these products are in place, the stronger the hold. If an adhesive is used as a temporary aid, which will later be removed by tearing or rinsing away, the removal process will be much easier with a short time span between adhering and removing.

Remember and apply this principle to save many unnecessary hours of tedious picking and removing of adhesive stabilizers.

Tear-Away Stablizer Hint

Whenever removing a tear-away stabilizer, tear at a 45° angle to the stitching line. Imagine tearing along the dotted line. This will prevent roughness and possible distortion of the stitches.

TROUBLESHOOTING - QUICK REFERENCE GUIDE

SKIPPED STITCHES

1. Change to a fresh needle. Sewing on synthetic fibers dulls the needle quicker than sewing on natural fibers.

2. Change to a larger size needle. A too small needle skips stitches for one of two reasons: If the needle shaft is too lightweight for the fabric, it deflects as it penetrates the fabric, moving it too far away from the bobbin to catch the bobbin thread and complete the stitch; or if the needle shaft and thread groove are too small, the fabric hugs the needle too tightly and doesn't allow the thread to form the loop necessary for the bobbin to catch it and create the stitch. Penetration with a larger size needle makes a bigger hole, creating more room for the thread to form the necessary loop.

3. If sewing on Lycra trim, change to a Stretch needle.

4. If sewing on an older machine it sometimes corrects the problem by using a very narrow zigzag stitch of .5 or 1mm in width, 3mm or longer in length.

5. If you just changed the needles and are suddenly experiencing skipped stitches, when you weren't experiencing this before, check to make sure the needle is inserted all the way up into the needle holder.

MACHINE BALKS AT FABRIC BULKINESS

1. Adjust for a longer stitch length.

2. Adjust the presser foot for a lighter pressure.

3. If you are sewing on a "relic" machine, it may require assistance feeding the fleece. Help with the feeding by using one hand to gently pull from behind and, with the other hand, push the fleece from the front. Do not distort the fabric, just help it.

RIPPLING OR DISTORTED SEAMS

1. Adjust for a longer stitch length.

2. Adjust the presser foot for a lighter pressure.

4. Set serger differential to 1 or 1.5.

5. Sew with a 5/8" seam allowance then trim to 1/4". The wider seam allowance allows for more contact between the presser foot, fabric and feed dogs. Alter the pattern if necessary.

SHIFTING OF FLEECE LAYERS

1. Adjust for a longer stitch length.

2. Adjust the presser foot for a lighter pressure.

3. Try a Walking foot or a Roller foot.

4. Sew with a 5/8" seam allowance then trim to 1/4". The wide seam allowance allows for more contact between the presser foot, fabric and feed dogs. Alter pattern if necessary.

BUCKLING ZIPPERS - FACT OF LIFE

It is virtually impossible to achieve perfectly flat zippers when sewing a bulky, stretchy fleece onto a rigid zipper tape.

Note: Don't be too hard on yourself. Check out the $200 jackets in ready-to-wear and you'll realize that you sew in a better zipper!

GOOD-LOOKING ZIPPER HINTS

1. Work on a flat surface. Lay the fleece at a 1:1 ratio onto the zipper tape. Do not stretch or force anything to fit!

2. Use wash-away basting tape to "baste" zipper in place.

3. Use a longer stitch length of 3mm to 3.5mm.

4. Lessen presser foot pressure.

5. If the fleece is quite bulky, consider using the Un-Traditional Blunt Edge method discussed in Part-6 under No-Hassle Zippers.

6. If frequently fighting the feed system on the machine and the Zipper foot is the narrow ski style, try using a regular presser foot. Move the needle position to the far right or the far left to stitch the zipper. This allows more contact between the presser foot, fabric, zipper tape and feed dogs.

PRINT IS OFF-GRAIN

Sometimes you'll find a beautiful print at a bargain price only to find that it was printed slightly off-grain. Unlike other fabrics, you can take advantage of the very forgiving nature of fleece and pile fabrics. Lay out the pattern pieces according to the print rather than the grain.

PART THREE

PATTERN CHOICES

The following are Tips & Hints to refer to when using patterns that are not specifically designed for polar fabrics.

Today we have many pattern choices for sewing fleece garments. The pattern companies have released patterns for everything from skiwear to pajamas, turtleneck pullovers, socks, mittens and hats. Even headbands and sweatpants patterns can be found. If you've seen it in ready-to-wear then rest assured that it can be found in a commercial pattern.

"But," you ask, "Can I use my "oldie-but-goodie" favorite from my private pattern stash?" The answer is "Of course!" This is a sewer's whole justification for stashing and hoarding mountains of patterns!

CHOOSING PATTERNS NOT SPECIFICALLY DESIGNED FOR FLEECES

The first consideration is the same as when sewing any garment: Choose a pattern that is appropriate for the fleece weight and the garment end use. There are so many weights of fleece now available that it is easy to find lighter weights that are perfect for turtlenecks, pajamas and even underwear. Middle weight fleeces are appropriate for "sweatsuit" use and hefty, beefy weights are for weather-beater outdoor use.

If the fleece is lighter weight, pretend that it is an interlock T-shirting fabric. Choose a pattern and construct the garment as usual. If choosing a heavy weight fleece, choose a pattern with more ease such as a sweatshirt style or loose jacket.

GENERAL GUIDELINES

Choose a pattern with simple lines and few details. Avoid a lot of seamlines, top-stitch detailing or curves that require "easing-in." Polar garments are casual and sporty, not tailored in nature.

SLEEVE CAP CONSIDERATIONS

For best results with mid-weight to heavy fleeces, choose a pattern with a dropped shoulder line; for example a "sweatshirt style" and a flatter sleeve cap.

A higher sleeve cap is usually marked with a single notch indicating the front and a double notch indicating the back. The high sleeve cap is intended to be first gathered, then sewn into the armhole.

The flatter sleeve cap eases into the dropped shoulder line armscye without a need for gathering. *Note: Gathering is too bulky for fleece.*

SIZING CONSIDERATIONS

If choosing a fleece that is thicker than the fabrics recommended on the pattern envelope, consider the bulk of the fleece as taking up one whole size. To compensate, make the pattern one size larger.

If you are choosing a sweatshirt pattern that was intended to be worn "as a sweatshirt" and the goal is to make it out of a heavy fleece to wear as outerwear: Step up one size to compensate for the bulk of the fleece. Step up a second size because the garment will be worn over another layer of clothing.

In other words, if "changing the rules," consider how the fit of the garment may be affected and make appropriate size changes.

Note: It's not hard... just logical.

SIMPLE DESIGN CHANGES

Nancy's Motto: Plan ahead with simple pattern changes to make your sewing life easier and your garments look sharper.

COLOR-BLOCKING

Today's pullovers, jackets and vests can offer a dynamic look with the simple use of color blocking. *Any one-color garment can easily and quickly be changed to a multi-color outfit. Look in better stores and catalogs to get ideas, grab a pencil and ruler and begin creating the same designer looks!*

COLOR-BLOCKING GUIDELINES

1. Choose a garment with relatively simple lines. Don't add more seamlines to a garment that already has quite a bit of detailing.
2. Trace the full pattern onto pattern tracing material and mark in the straight-of-grain line.
3. Pencil sketch potential color-block lines.

Simple Principle Note: Place color-block lines at a flattering location for your particular figure type. Color-block lines command visual attention. Planned placement of color-block lines can achieve a variety of affects.

• Visually minimize the bust by placing a horizontal color-block line above the fullest part of the bust. This will essentially frame the face.

• To visually enlarge the bust, place a horizontal color-block line directly across the fullest part of the bust.
• Create vertical color-block lines to lengthen or add height.
• To visually minimize hip width, color-block the bottom of a jacket or pullover into

multiple color sections across the lower edge. Add one or more sections to match the pant color.

• Visually enlarge the hip width by creating a color-block on the lower edge of a jacket or pullover. Use a contrasting solid color band that does not match the pant color.

• When using "V" color-block lines, the open part of the "V" visually widens an area. The point of the "V" narrows an area. A "V" open at the shoulders and tapering to a point at the hem, visually widens the shoulders and narrows the hips. A "V" with the point at the neck and the opening at the lower edge visually narrows the shoulders and widens the hips.

Horizontal color-block lines have the tendency to shorten, especially if the color intensities are uneven.

4. To avoid unnecessary seam bulk, do not end color-block seamlines at an underarm point, shoulder point, shoulder/neck point or a place with multiple seams.

5. Plan color-block lines accordingly if the garment neck edge is to be trimmed as part of the pattern construction.

COLOR-BLOCKING HOW-TO'S

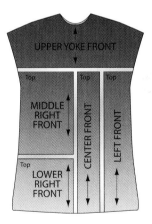

1. Draw color-block lines where desired.
2. Draw straight-of-grain lines in each color-block section.
3. Completely label each section: Upper Right, Middle Left, Lower Left, Top edge, Bottom edge, etc. Also, label the color from which the pieces will be cut.

4. When cutting fabric, cut a single layer with **fabric right side up** and **pattern piece right side up**. It is important to remember to add for seam allowances to both sides of the cut-apart color-block lines.

5. Sew color-block pieces together to form one whole front (back, sleeve, etc.)

NANCY'S HINT:

For an easy way to remind yourself to add the necessary seam allowances, before cutting the newly drawn pattern apart, draw a bold wavy line over all the color-block lines. Along the side of the wavy lines, write 1/4" or 5/8". These wavy lines act as a reminder to add the appropriate seam allowances when cutting out the fabric.

NANCY'S HINT:

If the color-blocking is quite involved, before you begin sewing, lay out all the pieces together like a jigsaw puzzle, then sew.

COLOR-BLOCK SEWING

Make sure you add the proper seam allowance for the seam method chosen. Seam options include traditional seams, edge-stitched or top-stitched, serged edge, cover-stitched or flatlocked.

NANCY'S RESCUE HINT:

You cut out all the color blocks and just realized you forgot to add the seam allowance?

1. Use a edge-stitch presser foot as a centering guide and simply butt the color-block sections next to each other.

2. Use a wide and long multiple zigzag stitch or serpentine stitch (4mm X 4mm minimum) to sew the sections together.

3. Leave seams "as is" or over-lay seams with edge-stitched decorative trim strips of ribbon or UltraSuede.

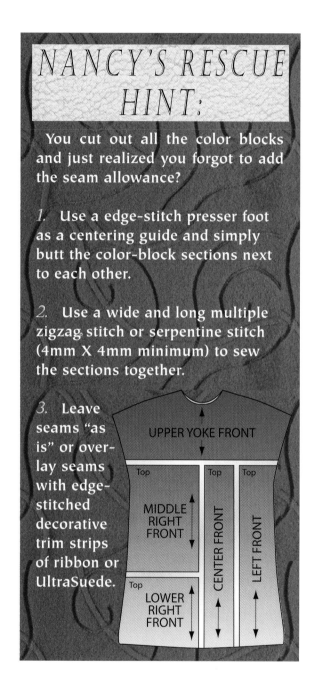

UPPER YOKE FRONT

Top — MIDDLE RIGHT FRONT

Top — CENTER FRONT

Top — LEFT FRONT

Top — LOWER RIGHT FRONT

COPY-CAT DESIGNER COLLAR

Since so many of today's garments are color-blocked, this collar detailing is the perfect finishing touch. On a color-blocked garment, a color-blocked collar adds interest and offers an opportunity to place the most flattering color next to the face. Choose a pattern that features a zipper-through-the-collar design. This feature enables the garment be zipped up or worn open with a turndown collar.

Something to think about...

Directions are given as though the collar will be worn zipped up to the top, turtleneck fashion. The inner collar is higher than the outer collar.

When worn zipped up, 3/4" of the contrasting inner collar curls up and over the top edge to create a color band.

If the collar will always be worn unzipped and folded open, reverse the inner collar and the outer collar pattern pieces. **Inner collar** will be the shorter dimension and **outer collar** will be the wider dimension.

(The contrast color will show with the collar worn open.)

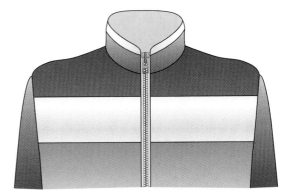

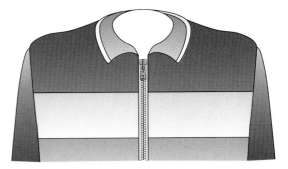

DRAFTING THE COPY CAT DESIGNER COLLAR

1. Standing a tape measure on edge, measure entire **front** and **back** neck edge on the seamline of the pattern pieces. For example, if a pattern calls for 1/4" seam allowance at the neckline, measure on the1/4" seamline. If a pattern calls for 5/8" neck seamline, measure on the 5/8" seam-line. From the total measurement taken, subtract 1" (for 1/4" seam allowance garment) or subtract 2 1/2" (for 5/8" seam allowance garment).

2. Draw **outer collar** 2 3/4" high x deter-mined length (above). Label as **outer collar**.

3. Draw **inner collar** 4 1/4" high x deter-mined length (above). Label as **inner collar**.

4. **Right** sides together, using a 1/4" seam, sew **inner collar** (higher collar) to **outer collar** (shorter collar) along one long edge. Press seam allowances towards **outer collar**.

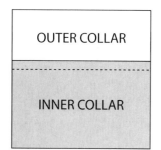

5. Fold collar in half, **wrong** sides together and press.

6. With collar still folded in half, trim both ends.

Begin 1/2" at the fold and taper to nothing at the raw

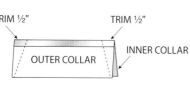

edges. This slight amount of shaping prevents flaring of the stand-up collar.

7. Follow the pattern directions for zipper insertion and finishing stitching.

NO-FAIL COLLAR CHANGE

A very popular style on jackets and vests is the zipper-through-the-collar design. However, the squared collar points require that sewing is "right on the money" for the points to look matched and even. If you are the slightest bit "off" in matching the corners, it will be like wearing a neon sign blaring: "Error! Error! Tear out and re-do." (Sewers hate that!) Slightly rounding off the corners and lowering the zipper placement offers welcome "grace room" so that a slight mis-match will not be obvious.

1. Before beginning construction, slightly round off the upper collar points.
Note: This is where the zipper was to end.

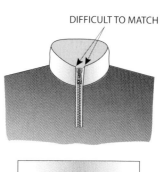

ORIGINAL COLLAR PATTERN PIECE

"REVISED" COLLAR PATTERN PIECE

2. When inserting the zipper, place the upper end of the zipper 1/2" below the curved top edge.

This simple pattern change gives great looking zippered collars every time!

ELIMINATING SEPARATE

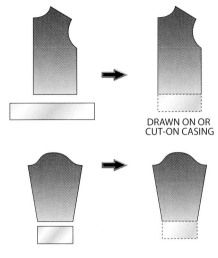

DRAWN ON OR
CUT-ON CASING

ELASTIC CASINGS

If the pattern features a separate bottom band with encased elastic; and separate cuff bands with encased elastic; eliminate excess seam allowance bulk by converting to cut-on casings.

Cut-On Casing

1. Lengthen lower edge of garment or sleeve 2 x elastic width plus 1/2".
For example, a pattern calls for 1 1/4" Action Elastic encased in a separate band. The garment should be lengthened by 3".
Note: 1 1/4" x 2 + 1/2" = 3".
2. Leaving an opening to insert elastic, fold up hem 1 1/2" and top-stitch along the upper edge to secure.
3. Insert elastic.
4. Pull elastic to desired length and secure at both ends.
5. Stretching elastic to fit, use a long stitch length (4mm or longer) and sew one or two rows of stitching down the center of the hem allowance. Generously steam to return elastic to original dimension. *Caution: Do not place iron onto the fleece.*
See Part Five for more detailed instructions on sewing elastic.

NO SIDE-SEAM JACKETS AND VESTS

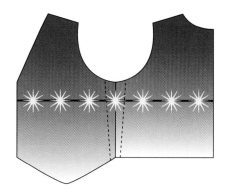

There will be many times when you will be working with a dramatic print, a definite grooved texture or a plush design. Side seams are often too bulky, distort the prints or interrupt the texture. Jackets and vests look much sharper without a side seam!

HOW TO ELIMINATE THE SIDE SEAMS

1. Overlap the **front** and **back** jacket or vest pattern pieces at the underarm points. Overlap 1 1/4" if the pattern calls for 5/8" seam allowances or 1/2" if the pattern calls for 1/4" seam allowance.

2. Adjust the amount of overlap at the bottom edge of the garment so that the center back fold line is parallel to the front straight-of-grain lines.

Note: The overlap may be less at the bottom edge than at the underarm edge.

3. Cut out the jacket or vest in one piece.

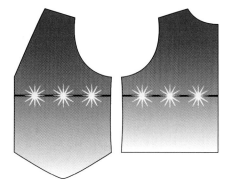

It is necessary to use a pattern with relatively straight side seams and no side seam pockets. If the pattern includes side seam pockets, eliminate them. If pockets are desired, create welt or patch pockets. This idea does not work if it is necessary to have side seams for pockets or other design details.

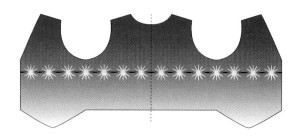

SEWING CHANGES

When it comes time to sew the sleeves into a jacket, sew the underarm sleeve seam and set the sleeve into the jacket armhole. *Note: This may be a minor change from the pattern directions. Although minor in the sewing process it is definitely worth the change!*

PART FOUR
SEAM OPTIONS

The choices are many when sewing with fleece and pile fabrics. Opt for traditional seams or take advantage of the wonderful no-fray characteristics these fabrics possess. Have some fun!

When sewing with pile fabrics such as Berber, shearling or plush, the nap may get caught in the seamline. Use a toothbrush or your fingernail and "scratch" on the seamline. This will draw out the nap and make the seamline almost invisible.

A 5/8" SEAM ALLOWANCE PATTERN...

"COOPERATIVE SEAMS"

If you are sewing with a conventional sewing machine, sew a 5/8" seam allowance. If the seam allowance is "cooperative" and lays nice and flat without "springing up," simply finger press the seam allowances flat.

"UNCOOPERATIVE SEAMS"

If the seam allowance is "uncooperative" and wants to "spring up," double-stitch the seam and trim close to the second stitching.

"DOUBLE TOP-STITCH"

If sewing with a dense, flat fleece, you may prefer the effect of top-stitching at 1/4" along both sides of the seamline. Finger press 5/8" seam allowance open and top-stitch at 1/4" along both sides of the seam. Use double top-stitching as a nice finishing detail or to tame uncooperative seam allowances.

"MOCK FLAT FELLED" TECHNIQUE

Another nice way to tame "uncooperative" seam allowances.

Using a conventional sewing machine and sew a 5/8" seam allowance.

Trim only one seam allowance to a generous 1/8."

Finger press the remaining full-width seam allowance over the trimmed seam allowance.

Top-stitch 1/4" away from seamline.

If desired, trim excess seam allowance close to top-stitching line.

On non-textured fleeces, the trimmed seam allowance fills the top-stitched area and creates a nice looking, slightly raised welt.

SERGING 5/8" SEAMS

Simply trim off 3/8" as you sew.

A 1/4" SEAM ALLOWANCE PATTERN...

Sew with a conventional sewing machine or serger. A nice finishing touch is created by finger pressing the seam allowances to one side and top-stitching.

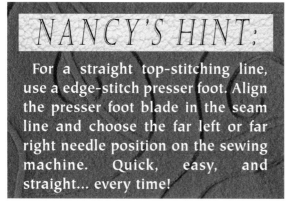

NANCY'S HINT:

For a straight top-stitching line, use a edge-stitch presser foot. Align the presser foot blade in the seam line and choose the far left or far right needle position on the sewing machine. Quick, easy, and straight... every time!

NANCY'S HINT FOR AVOIDING DROOPING SHOULDERS

Some fleece happens to have a lot of cross-grain stretch, without good recovery. This is often found with inexpensive goods. Prevent the shoulder seams from growing by incorporating clear elastic into the seamline as you sew.

1. Cut a piece of 1/4" or 3/8" clear elastic the length of the shoulder line.
Note: Measure the shoulder line on the pattern piece, not the cut-out fabric. The cut-out fabric may have already grown in the cutting and handling process.
2. When beginning to sew the shoulder seam, slip the elastic under the presser foot and take a couple of stitches to anchor the elastic to the seam.
3. As you sew, incorporate the elastic in stitching. Stretching the elastic to match the fabric shoulder length. When finished, the elastic will draw up to the original intended pattern fit.

This technique works with conventional sewing machines or sergers.

Note: I prefer clear elastic rather than stay tape. Clear elastic allows the shoulder seam to "give" like the rest of the garment and it does not add bulk to the seam.

Hint: For an easier way to sew clear elastic into a shoulder seam, cut the elastic 2" longer than necessary. This will give a 1" elastic tail at the beginning and end of the seamline, making it easier to handle.

LAPPED SEAMS

Fleece and pile fabrics don't ravel and thicker fabrics maintain a nice, clean, blunt edge when cut with a rotary cutter. Take advantage of these characteristics to eliminate bulk when sewing seams, pockets and collars.

If less bulk is preferred on a traditional shoulder seam, shawl collar seam, center back seam or a side seam, take advantage of fleece's no-ravel feature and lap the seams. They will be nice and flat with little bulk.

1. Overlap 1 1/4" for a 5/8" seam allowance or overlap 1/2" for a 1/4" seam allowance.

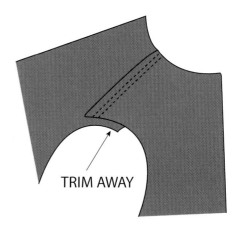

TRIM AWAY

2. Tape overlapped fabrics in place, using 1/4" wash-away basting tape.
Note: There is no need to remove basting tape as it will wash away in the first laundering.

3. Sew lapped seams in one of the following ways:

   • Use a conventional sewing machine to edge-stitch and then top-stitch in place.

   • Use a conventional sewing machine with a 4.0 or 6.0 double needle to stitch in place.

   • Use a cover-stitch machine to stitch in place.

4. Trim, if necessary, to create neat edges. (See illustration on previous page.)

BLUNT-EDGED PATCH POCKETS

When applying patch pockets made from thicker fabrics, you will delight in the nice blunt cut edge that remains when the fabric piece has been cut out with a rotary cutter.

When applying patch pockets to a garment, simply sew the pockets flat onto the garment and leave the raw outer edges exposed! *Note: Turning under the outer edges and stitching in place will result in bulky, uneven edges.*

1. Trim the seam allowance from the side and lower edges of the pocket.

2. Turn under the facing at upper edge and stitch in place.

3. On the **wrong** side of the pocket, apply wash-away basting tape around outer edges of the pocket.

4. Adhere to garment.

5. Edge-stitch and top-stitch in place.

   Note: Couldn't be easier! And it looks great too!

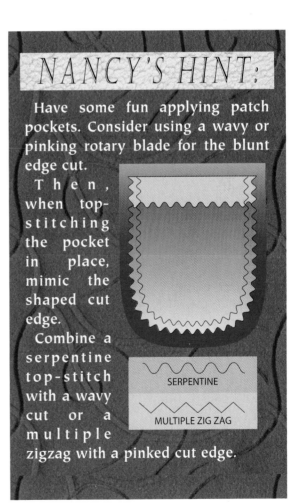

NANCY'S HINT:

Have some fun applying patch pockets. Consider using a wavy or pinking rotary blade for the blunt edge cut. Then, when top-stitching the pocket in place, mimic the shaped cut edge. Combine a serpentine top-stitch with a wavy cut or a multiple zigzag with a pinked cut edge.

SERPENTINE

MULTIPLE ZIG ZAG

BLUNT-EDGED COLLARS

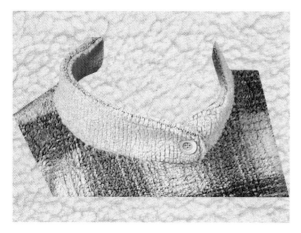

If, after rotary cutting, the fleece has a crisp blunt edge, it will work well when sewing a traditional turn-down collar or a sporty stand-up collar. Try this no-bulk technique:

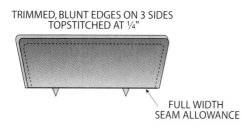

TRIMMED, BLUNT EDGES ON 3 SIDES
TOPSTITCHED AT ¼"

FULL WIDTH
SEAM ALLOWANCE

1. If pattern calls for a 5/8" seam allowance, trim 3/8" from outer edges for a 1/4" seam allowance. Do not trim the collar edge that will be sewn to the neckline.

2. Pin the collars **wrong** sides together.

3. Sew collars together by top-stitching 1/4" around the outer edges.

4. If necessary, use a rotary cutter to "clean up" the raw edges.

5. Follow the pattern directions for sewing the collar to the neck edge.

This technique eliminates all the bulk that would result from seam allowances turned to the inside of the collar. Not only less bulky, but quicker, too!

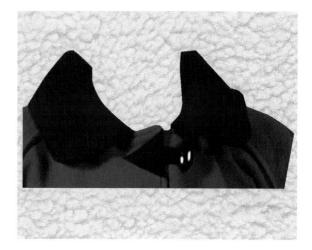

Note: If the fleece is double-sided and heavy enough, consider using a single layer of fabric and a blunt edge finish for the collar and cuffs. However, experiment first, and make sure it has enough density and body to work well with just one layer.

PART FIVE

READY TO WEAR EDGE FINISH TECHNIQUES

Sewing is fun when you can copy ready-to-wear techniques to reproduce the style of an "expensive" designer. The edge finishes discussed in this chapter are made similar to those found in better ready-to-wear garments. Also included are practical solutions to "real life" situations that may be encountered.

In the not so distant past, all jackets and tops were customarily finished with ribbing at the cuffs and lower edge. Recently major sportswear companies, like Patagonia and Columbia, introduced finishing garments with a narrow Lycra wrapped edge finish. Home sewers can duplicate this style in two ways: **The Hard Way** which is the "real" way or, my personal favorite, **The Cheater's Way**! The Cheater's Way is easy, fast and the outcome is better.

A WORD ABOUT LYCRA TRIM

The first two techniques use 2" strips of nylon Lycra (swimwear), with the greater stretch going in the length of the strip. The right side of this fabric has a shine and the wrong side has a matte finish. Depending on the desired appearance, either side can be used. The color tone frequently varies from the right to the wrong side. Cotton/Lycra may also be used.

Thankfully a number of suppliers now offer pre-cut, packaged Lycra trim strips. Make sure the pre-cut trim strips are 2" wide. Some are only 1 3/4" wide which is too narrow and too difficult with which to work. A five yard length will be enough for just about any project.

If pre-cut strips are not available at your favorite store custom create trim strips as follows:

1. Purchase one yard of nylon/Lycra swimwear.
2. Cut 2" strips of fabric with the greater stretch going the length of the strip.
Note: On nylon/Lycra fabrics, greater stretch is usually on the lengthwise grain, parallel to the selvage. This is opposite to other stretch fabrics.

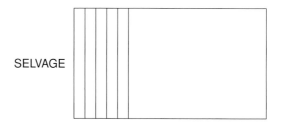

SELVAGE

3. Place strips **right** sides together and stitch a bias seam.

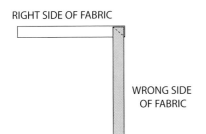

RIGHT SIDE OF FABRIC

WRONG SIDE OF FABRIC

4. Trim seam allowance.

5. Finger press seam allowance open.

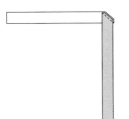

6. Continue splicing until strip is long

enough to encompass all garment edges.

Refer to this section every time you begin a new project!

If using a commercial pattern that features a similar edge finish, substitute with one of the edge finishes discussed below. Follow the pattern's order of sewing construction.

If you plan to venture out and add designer details, some planning is required before you begin:

1. Decide where the edge finish will be applied. Will it be around the entire garment, around the center front only, around the armholes or collar edge?

2. Determine the required trim length. Splice more than enough trim to finish all the edges. This allows splicing seams to be placed at inconspicuous places.

3. Decide what will be applied at the corners.

Center Front - If there will be trim on both the center front edges and on the bottom edge, completely finish the bottom edge first. Then, apply the trim to the center front edges. Tuck the trim ends under at the bottom edge to finish the front squared edge.

Collars - If trim is to go around sharp corners, it is better to round off the collar points rather than miter the trim. *(See No-Fail Collar Change in Part 3)*

Vest Points - Slightly soften the points to make the trim application easy and more consistent.

4. Plan the "order of sewing construction" to eliminate bulk and create as few trim seams as possible. For example, there are three ways to sew trim to a vest armhole:

A. Sew the shoulder and the side seams and apply the edge finish to the armhole.

This entails applying the trim to the armhole, which is an enclosed circle. This would be an awkward beginning and ending with a bulky, difficult finish to the ends of the trim.

B. Sew the shoulder seam. Completely apply the edge finish. Sew the side seam. This results in a thick, bulky underarm seam through the trim and unfinished trim ends.

C. Sew the shoulder seam. Sew only the first step of the trim application to the armhole edge. Sew the side seam up to and through the end of the trim strip. Wrap and finish stitching the trim. The result will be a flat trim seam with finger-pressed-open seams and completely finished edges.

Note: Choice "C" is by far the best approach because it is the easiest and least bulky method with no unfinished trim edges. For a complete, detailed order of sewing, see the section Self-Fabric Wrapped Edges – A.K.A. Fat Piping.

WRAPPED EDGES

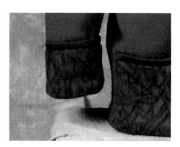

For purposes of instruction here, we will picture a straight edge. This could represent the center front

edge of a jacket, vest armholes, the outer edges of collars, the lower edges of sleeves or the lower edges of garments. See the end of each section for specific cuff and bottom finish applications.

The final appearance on all of the following applications are the same. The difference lies in the type of trim used and the application techniques utilized.

LYCRA WRAPPED EDGES-THE HARD WAY

THE "REAL" WAY

I call this the "hard" way because it is time-consuming and tricky to achieve symmetrical top-stitching. I include this technique because it is the "real" way manufacturers do it. Don't be too critical of your end results! Go check out ready-to-wear and you will find that their top-stitching isn't perfect either!

1. Cut center front edge, armhole edge, sleeve edge, etc. to the finished depth. *Note: Unlike a hem in which the finished edge is shorter than the cut edge, with wrapped edges the width or length will not be changed. The raw edge of the fabric will simply be wrapped with the trim. If there is a seam allowance or hem allowance, cut garment edge to the finished depth.*

2. Fold the 2" Lycra trim strip in half lengthwise and press in the fold. This pressing step is important because it creates a sharp edge for wrapping later.

3. Work from the **wrong** side of the garment. Align both raw edges of the folded Lycra strip to the raw edge of garment and pin in place.

4. With a serger, sew Lycra trim to the garment. Use an exact 1/4" seam allowance. Place garment against machine with trim strip on top. Do not trim off any fabric or Lycra trim.

Wrong Side of Fabric

This technique can be done on a conventional sewing machine. However, it is better sewn on a serger because the seam allowance is consistent and the serger overcast stitching compacts the fluffy seam allowances, making it easier to wrap the trim. If a serger is not available, use a conventional sewing machine and sew a meticulous 1/4" seam allowance. Then to flatten, zigzag stitch the seam allowance area.

Now comes the "fun" part.

5. Wrap the folded pressed edge of the Lycra trim to the **right** side of the garment. Wrap it up, over and around, encasing Lycra raw edges and the fleece raw edge. Pin so that the fold just covers the first stitching line.

Right Side of Fabric

NANCY'S HINT:

When sewing the trim to the center front edge, lower edges that are not gathered, or in any area that edges are to lay flat, slightly tug the Lycra trim while sewing. This will prevent rippling or buckling when wrapping the trim to the finished position. Don't stretch a lot...just a little. When applying trim to curves such as armholes and neck edges, moderately stretch the trim when sewing onto the garment. This will cause the trim to "hug" the neck or armhole, rather than "fan out."

NANCY'S HINT:

Use tons and tons of pins. Pin every 1/2" at right angles to the fold.

6. Sewing from the **right** side of the garment, using a Stretch or ballpoint needle and an edge-stitch presser foot, edge-stitch on the folded edge of the Lycra trim.

TO STITCH LIKE THIS

NANCY'S HINT:

Here's where you thank the sewing angels above that you have a newer sewing machine.

To make this step easier:

1. Use a edge-stitch presser foot.
2. Choose half-left or full-left needle position (or half-right or full-right).
3. Engage the "needle down" function on the sewing machine.
4. Sew slowly and meticulously. Edge-stitch on the folded edge of the Lycra trim. Frequently stop and re-align as you sew. Stop with the needle down as you reach and remove each pin. The point of a seam ripper is a good tool to use to keep the Lycra fold exactly in place.

For best results, sew slowly. This is not a "pedal to the metal" operation.

ZIPPER INSERTION BEHIND WRAPPED EDGES: SEE PART 6 – NO HASSLE ZIPPERS

GATHERING THE CUFFS & BOTTOM EDGE OF THE GARMENT

Lycra, with its strong elasticity and excellent recovery, has enough strength to gather up the cuff edges and lower edge for a snug fit.

CUFFS

Cut a 2" wide Lycra trim strip 7" to 7 1/2" long for a small adult size, 8" to 8 1/2" for a medium size or 9" to 9 1/2" for a large size. Apply in the same manner as the "Hard Way" above, except stretch the Lycra trim strip to match cuff edge.

BOTTOM FINISH

Cut a 2" wide Lycra trim strip 4" less than hip measurement. Divide the trim strip into quarters and mark with pins. Divide the lower edge of the garment into quarters and mark with pins. Match quarter marks and pin Lycra strip to the bottom edge of garment. Apply in the same manner as above. Stretch the Lycra trim strip to match the bottom edge of the garment.

LYCRA WRAPPED EDGES–
THE CHEATER'S WAY
THE EASY WAY

Right Side of Fabric

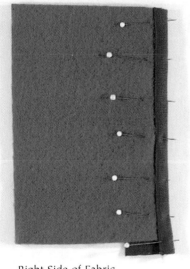

Right Side of Fabric

The finished appearance is better because it is easier to do the top-stitching! There is less bulk; three layers of Lycra as opposed to six layers in the "real" method. And...it's much quicker!

Note: Lycra trim or ribbing yardage can be used for the Cheater's Way. Lycra was pictured in the Hard Way illustrations and ribbing is pictured for the Cheater's Way illustrations. Compare the finished appearances.

1. Cut center front edge, armhole edge, sleeve edge, etc. to the finished depth.

Note: Unlike a hem in which the finished edge is shorter than the cut edge, with wrapped edges the width or length will not be changed. The raw edge of the fabric will simply be wrapped with the trim. If there is a seam allowance or hem allowance, cut garment edge to the finished depth.

2. **Right** sides together, pin a **single** layer of 2" Lycra trim to the garment edge. Keep raw edges even.

3. With a serger, sew Lycra trim to the garment. Use an exact 1/4" seam allowance. Place garment against machine with trim strip on top. Do not trim off any fabric or Lycra trim.

This technique can be done on a conventional sewing machine. However, it is better sewn on a serger because the seam allowance is consistent and the serger stitching compacts the fluffy seam allowances, making it easier to wrap the trim. If a serger is not available, use a conventional sewing machine and sew a meticulous 1/4" seam allowance. Then, zigzag stitch the seam allowance area to flatten.

Now comes the easy part.

4. Wrap the Lycra trim strip to the **wrong** side of the garment. Wrap it up, over and around the raw edges. Encase the Lycra raw edge and the fleece raw edge. From the **right** side of the garment, pin trim strip in finished posi-

tion. Make sure the trim is even and consistent. Excess Lycra trim will overlap the stitching line on the **wrong** side.

5. Using an edgestitch presser foot for precision stitch placement, and sewing from the **right** side of the garment, stitch-in-the-ditch to secure wrapped trim strip on the backside.
(To stitch-in-the-ditch, sew exactly in the trim seamline.)

6. Use sharp scissors to cut excess Lycra trim close to the stitching.

WRONG SIDE OF FABRIC

ZIPPER INSERTION BEHIND WRAPPED EDGES: SEE PART 6 – NO HASSLE ZIPPERS.

GATHERING THE CUFFS AND BOTTOM EDGE OF GARMENT – THE CHEATER'S WAY

Lycra, with its strong elasticity and excellent recovery, has enough strength to gather up the cuff edges and the lower edge for a snug fit. If the fleece is a heavy weight and you question the strength of three layers of Lycra, use the "Ribbing With Elastic" technique and incorporate elastic in the trim.

CUFFS

Cut a 2" wide Lycra trim strip 7" to 7 1/2" long for a small adult size, 8" to 8 1/2" for a medium size or 9" to 9 1/2" for a large size. Apply according to "The Cheater's Way" instructions. Stretch the Lycra trim strip to match the cuff edge.

BOTTOM FINISH

Cut a 2" wide Lycra trim strip 5" to 6" less than hip measurement. Divide the trim strip into quarters and mark with pins. Divide the lower edge of the jacket into quarters and mark with pins. Match quarter marks and pin Lycra strip to the bottom edge of the garment. Apply in the same manner as above, stretching the Lycra trim strip to match the bottom edge of the garment.

RIBBING WRAPPED EDGES

This edge finish is the same as "The Cheater's Way" of applying Lycra trim, with the exception of using ribbing yardage rather than Lycra trim. Generally, it is easier to find a better selection of colors in ribbing yardage than in nylon Lycra. Ribbing is a delightful option to have available.

Ribbing wrapped edges are suitable for front edges, collars and armholes. It is not suitable for cuffs and lower edges that need to be gathered in for a snug fit. If it is necessary to gather the cuffs and lower edge, see the "Ribbing With Elastic" technique.

DETERMINING RIBBING YARDAGE REQUIREMENTS

1. Measure around all the edges to be wrapped. For example, center fronts, collar, bottom, armholes and cuffs.
2. Take this measurement and divide by the ribbing width (the minimum number of trim cuts required). Most ribbing is 32" to 60" wide.
3. Multiply by two. This is the width into which you will be cutting the strips.
4. Add 4" to allow "grace" room for place-

ment of splices at inconspicuous places, allowing for cuffs that use partial cuts, etc.

Example:

- Length of garment edges "to be wrapped" measures 140"(fronts + collar + bottom edge + cuffs).
- Ribbing is 36" wide.
  140" divided by 36" = 3.89.
  Round it up to 4 (4 full cuts required).
- 4 X 2" (width of strips) = 8" ribbing (minimum required).
- 8" + 4" ("grace room") = 12" ribbing (comfortable amount required to wrap the edges).

GATHERING THE CUFFS AND BOTTOM EDGE OF GARMENT

Ribbing alone does not have enough strength or sufficient recovery to gather fleece and pile fabrics, at the cuffs and lower edge, for a snug fit. To solve this situation, see "Ribbing with Elastic" technique.

ZIPPER INSERTION BEHIND WRAPPED EDGES: SEE PART 6 – NO HASSLE ZIPPERS

RIBBING WITH ELASTIC

RIBBING THAT ACTS LIKE LYCRA!
TO BE USED TO GATHER CUFFS AND LOWER EDGES

If using ribbing to wrap the edges of fabric you will need a little extra help in those areas that require a snug fit and need to be gathered. The solution is to simply incorporate 3/8" clear elastic into the seam allowance!

TO FINISH THE CUFFS

1. **Right** sides together, sew a single layer of 2" ribbing trim to the lower edges of sleeves. Use a 1/4" seam allowance.

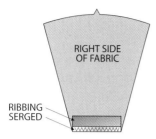

RIGHT SIDE OF FABRIC

RIBBING SERGED

2. Cut 3/8" clear elastic 7" to 7 1/2" long for a small adult size, 8" to 8 1/2" for a medium size or 9" to 9 1/2" for a large size. Stretch elastic to fit the bottom edge of the sleeve and zigzag stitch elastic onto the seam allowance area. Use a 4mm wide and 4mm long zigzag stitch. Although the 3/8" elastic is slightly wider than the 1/4" seam allowance, when stretched and stitched in place, it will fit perfectly.

3. Sew side seam and underarm seam of garment. Sew through to the end of the ribbing trim strip.

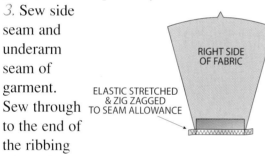

RIGHT SIDE OF FABRIC

ELASTIC STRETCHED & ZIG ZAGGED TO SEAM ALLOWANCE

4. Wrap ribbing trim to the **wrong** side of the garment. Wrap up, over and around the raw edges, encasing the seam allowance and the clear elastic.

5. From the **right** side of the garment, pin ribbing trim in finished position. Make sure that the trim is even and consistent. Excess ribbing trim will overlap the seamline on the **wrong** side.

6. Sew from the **right** side of the garment. To secure the wrapped trim on the backside, use an edge-stitch presser foot for precision stitch placement and stitch-in-the-ditch, sewing exactly in the trim seamline.

7. Use sharp scissors to cut excess trim close to the stitching.

TO FINISH THE BOTTOM EDGE OF GARMENT

These sewing directions are identical for finishing the cuffs.

1. Cut ribbing 2" wide x measurement of the lower edge of the garment.
2. **Right** sides together, sew a single layer of 2" ribbing trim to the lower edge of the garment. Use a 1/4" seam allowance
3. Cut 3/8" clear elastic for the bottom edge to a length of 5" to 6" less than your hip measurement.
4. Quarter elastic and mark quarter marks with pins.
5. Quarter bottom edge of the garment and indicate quarter marks with pins.
6. Match quarter marks and pin elastic to ribbing/garment seam allowance.
7. Stretch elastic to fit. Sew elastic to seam allowance using a wide, long zigzag stitch.
8 Wrap, stitch and trim according to cuff directions above.

SELF-FABRIC WRAPPED EDGES – A.K.A. (ALSO KNOWN AS) FAT PIPING

There are times when matching Lycra trim or ribbing can not be found.

Do not be thwarted in the quest for trim because "Fat Piping" comes to the rescue! It is not piping in the true sense of the word. However, the finished result is a raised, plump, corded-look edge...with

NANCY'S HINT:

Be religious about marking the right side of the fabric. Remember that the right and wrong sides behave differently after wearing and laundering. It may only be a little bit of trim, but sometimes the differences are quite dramatic!

no cording!

"Fat Piping" is an option to use around vest front and lower edges, neck edges, and armholes. It is not suitable for cuffs, lower edges or other areas that need to be gathered.

OTHER OPTIONS

1. If using a printed fleece, plan a flattering area of the print to be the visible part of the "Fat Piping."

CUTTING SELF-FABRIC TRIM

From fleece self-fabric, cut a piece 2 1/2" wide by the length required to wrap and finish the garment edge. The greater stretch should be in the length of the strip.

If necessary, splice trim to get the necessary length. Refer to the "Splicing Directions" given for Lycra trim at the beginning of this chapter.

2. If the print is a striped pattern and enough fabric is available, cut the strips on the bias for an interesting effect.

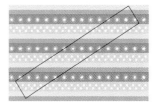

"Fat Piping" application method is similar to "The Cheater's Way" of applying Lycra wrapped edge, with a few minor exceptions:

1. Cut, to the finished depth, the center front edge, armhole edge, sleeve edge, etc.

Note: Unlike a hem, where the finished edge is shorter than the cut edge, using fat piping the width or length will not be changed. The raw edge of the fabric will simply be wrapped with the self-fabric trim. If there is a seam allowance or hem allowance, cut garment to finished depth.

2. **Right** sides together, pin a single layer of self-fabric trim strip to the garment. Keep the raw edges even.

3. Place garment against machine with trim strip on top. Sew with an exact 3/8" seam allowance.

Now comes the easy part.

4. Wrap the self-fabric trim strip to the **wrong** side of the garment. Wrap up, over and around, encasing the self-fabric raw edge and the garment raw edge. Working from the **right** side of the

garment, pin the trim strip in finished position. Make sure the trim is even and consistent. Excess trim will overlap the stitching line on the **wrong** side.

5. Using an edgestitch presser foot for precision stitch placement, and sewing from the right side of the garment, stitch-in-the-ditch to secure wrapped trim strip on the backside. (To stitch-in-the-ditch, sew exactly in the trim seamline.)

6. Use sharp scissors to cut excess trim close to the stitching line.

When wrapping and enclosing the seam allowances, the fluffiness of the fleece "plumps" the wrap and results in a 1/2" fat piping appearance.

ORDER OF SEWING

Think ahead and plan the order of construction to eliminate as many seams as possible when sewing Fat Piping or "The Cheater's Way" Lycra trim. As an example, if using "Fat Piping" as a finishing method on a vest, following are two examples of planned "good order of sewing":

FAT PIPING ON A VEST WITH SIDE SEAMS

1. Sew the **left** shoulder seam.

2. Sew the self-fabric trim to the **left** armhole.

3. Finger press the self-fabric trim away from the garment (towards the armhole opening).

4. Sew the **left** side seam. Sew up through unfinished edge of trim.

5. Wrap and finish the **left** armhole trim. Trim excess strip.

6. Sew **right** shoulder seam.

7. Sew the self-fabric trim to the **right** armhole.

8. **Right** sides together, begin on the **back** at the **un-sewn right side seam**. Sew the self-fabric trim across the **back**, across the **left front**, up the **left center front**, around the **neck edge**, down the

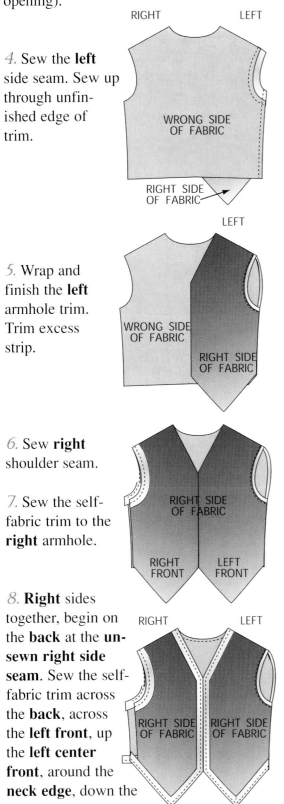

right center front and across the **right front** ending at the **right un-sewn side seam**.

9. Finger press self-fabric trim away from the garment at the hem edge and at the **right** armhole.

10. Sew **right** side seam. Sew from the unfinished edge of trim at the bottom, up the side seam and through to the unfinished edge of armhole trim.

11. Wrap and finish **right** armhole trim. Trim excess strip.

12. Wrap and finish outer edge trim. Trim excess strip.

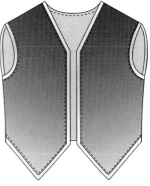

This order of sewing results in only three seams in the trim: **left** underarm, **right** underarm and lower **right** side seam.

If it is necessary to splice trim strip to go around the entire outer edge of the vest, the splice should be placed at an inconspicuous place, probably somewhere on the back of the garment.

FAT PIPING ON A NO SIDE–SEAM VEST

1. Sew the self-fabric trim to the **left** armhole.

2. Finger press the self-fabric trim away from the garment (towards the armhole opening).

3. Sew the **left** shoulder seam (from neck edge through unfinished edge of trim).

4. Wrap and finish the **left** armhole. Trim excess strip.

5. Repeat steps #1 and #2 for the **right** armhole.

6. **Right** sides together, begin at the **un-sewn right shoulder seam**, sew the self-fabric trim to the **right vest front**, across the **right front lower edge**, around the **back**, across the **left front lower edge**, up the **left front**, around the **back neck edge** and end at the **un-sewn right shoulder edge**. If necessary, splice trim for extra length. Splicing directions are found at the beginning of this section.

7. Finger press self-fabric trim away from the garment.

8. Sew **right** shoulder seam. Sew from the unfinished edge of trim at the armhole, through the garment shoulder to the unfinished edge of trim at the neck edge.

9. Wrap and finish the **right** armhole. Trim excess strip.

10. Wrap and finish the outer edge. Trim excess strip.

WIMPY RIBBING DILEMMA

There is no getting around the fact that, at some point in time, you are going to find a perfect once-in-a-lifetime ribbing match for a coveted piece of fleece...and it will be too lightweight to do the job properly!

Again, don't be defeated, there are a couple of simple remedies for this situation:

REMEDY # 1: DOUBLE UP!

Instead of using "the usual" 6" of ribbing which is sewn into a circle, folded in half to 3" and sewn to the sleeve edge, use 12" of ribbing...sewn into a circle, folded in half to 6" and folded in half

again to 3"! There now are four layers of ribbing to do the work of two!

This will make the once "wimpy" ribbing a little more rugged, heavier and more suitable for application to heavy fleece. *Note: This trick also works for the ribbing at the garment lower edge.*

REMEDY # 2: "ELASTICATE" IT!

To prevent sagging cuff edge, incorporate clear elastic next to the foldline.

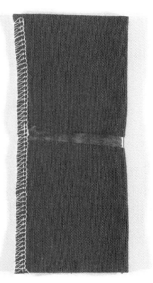

1. Cut ribbing for cuffs according to pattern directions and sew into a circle.

2. **Wrong** sides out, fold ribbing in half and mark the halfway foldline with a fabric pencil.

3. Using a 1:1 ratio, lay 3/8" or 1/2" clear elastic next to the foldline, encircling the ribbing.

4. Sew both ends of the elastic to the seamline.

When folding ribbing cuff in half to finished position, the elastic will lay alongside the foldline and keep the cuff in shape.

SELF-FABRIC TRIM

Don't overlook using self-fabric instead of ribbing for the cuffs and the lower bottom band. Fleeces frequently have quite a bit of stretch, sometimes on both the lengthwise and the crosswise grain. Cut the cuffs and lower band with the greater stretch going in the length. Cuffs and bottom bands are generally 6" to 8" wide and are folded in half to 3" or 4" wide.

CUFFS

Instead of using a specific measurement, wrap the self-fabric trim around your fist. Cut the trim long enough to comfortably slip your hand though. Add 1/2" for seam allowance.

BOTTOM BAND

Again, instead of using a specific measurement, wrap the self-fabric trim around your hips. Cut the trim long enough for a comfortable fit. Add 1/2" for seam allowance.

SELF-FABRIC CUFFS AND BOTTOM BAND

Sew to the garment in the usual manner.

NANCY'S HINT:

Self-fabric trim does not provide the same amount of stretch and recovery as "real" ribbing or Lycra. Don't stretch the self-fabric trim too hard when sewing it onto the garment. Generally, to gather the garment edge, ribbing is stretched when sewn onto the garment. When using self-fabric trim, first run gathering stitches along the garment edges and gather. Apply the trim, stretching only a moderate amount. When sewing self-fabric trim to garment, use a 3mm or longer stitch length.

"BACKWARDS" TOP-STITCHING

There are many times when a simple "turn under and top-stitch" will do the trick to finish the edge of a vest, cardigan, scarf, hood, etc. For an easy "turn under," and an accurate top-stitch that requires no trimming afterwards, **do it backwards**!

1. With the **right** side of the garment against the machine, and the **wrong** side facing up, turn up 1/2" to 5/8" hem.
2. If necessary, soften garment points for easier maneuvering.
3. Align the **left** edge of the presser foot along the raw edge of the fleece hem.
4. Move needle position to the **left**.
5. Top-stitch using a 3mm or longer stitch length.

Because the hem is being turned up as you go and everything is in plain sight, the hem will be even and the stitching will be consistent. There is no need to go back and trim "excesses" or re-stitch "misses." The bobbin stitch will be on the right side of the garment. Even if the bobbin stitch is not as pretty as the needle stitch, it won't matter because it sinks into the loft of the fleece!

ELASTIC CUFFS & HEMS

For those times when Lyrca or ribbing finish isn't desired or when colors don't match, cuffs and hems may be gathered using elastic. Choose a narrow finish or a wide sporty finish.

NANCY'S HINT:

For the best performance, choose high quality elastics. Inferior quality elastic does not have sufficient recovery to handle fleece.

Depending upon the elastic application, use a wide long zigzag stitch (4mm x 4mm) or a long straight stitch (4mm). Short stitches pile in too much thread. Short stitches will force the elastic to grow and does not allow it to return to its original dimension.

NARROW ELASTIC FINISH

Use 3/8" clear elastic or 3/8" cotton braid swimwear elastic.

CUFFS

1. Cut sleeve length 3/8" longer than desired finished length.
2. Cut elastic length 7" to 7 1/2" for an adult small size, 8" to 8 1/2" for a medium size or 9" to 9 1/2" for a large size.
3. Lap elastic 1/2" and sew into a circle.

4. Use a wide long zigzag stitch and sew elastic to the **wrong** side of sleeve edge stretching elastic to fit.

5. Turn up 3/8" hem, encasing elastic. Stitch with a wide long zigzag or serpentine stitch. Take care that the finishing stitching completely covers the edge of the elastic. This step will prevent it from curling outwards.

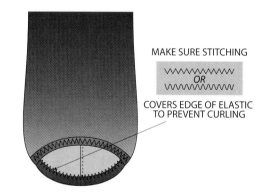

MAKE SURE STITCHING

OR

COVERS EDGE OF ELASTIC TO PREVENT CURLING

BOTTOM HEMS

1. Cut garment length 3/8" longer than desired finished length.
2. Cut elastic length 4" to 5" less than hip measurement.
3. Lap elastic 1/2" and sew into a circle.

4. Divide lower edge of garment into quarters and mark with pins.

5. Divide elastic into quarters and mark with pins.

6. Match quarter marks and sew elastic to the **wrong** side of garment using a wide, long zigzag stitch, stretching elastic to fit.

7. Turn up 3/8" hem encasing elastic. Stitch with a wide, long zigzag or serpentine stitch. Take care that the finishing stitching completely covers the edge of the elastic. This step will prevent it from curling outwards.

NANCY'S HINT:

Safety Idea: This elastic application is also a terrific way to gather in the edge of a hood on a child's garment. It eliminates a potentially dangerous drawcord around the child's neck and it fits snug enough to keep out the wind and the cold!

1. Measure against the child. Measure elastic from the center front edge of the neck, up and over the head and back around to center front neck edge. Allow for the amount of the hood edge you prefer to "snug up" around the child's face.

2. Zigzag elastic to the wrong side of hood edge.

3 Turn under 3/8" hem encasing elastic. Zigzag to finish

WIDER SPORTY ELASTIC FINISH

Use 1 1/4" Action Elastic.

Note: Action Elastic is a special sport elastic that retains its shape and memory after it is stitched through. Do not use "pajama" elastic because it is too soft.

CUFFS

1. Cut sleeve length 1 3/4" longer than desired finished sleeve length.

2. Cut elastic length wrist measurement and add 1 1/2"

3. Sew sleeve underarm seam according to pattern directions.

4. Turn up 1 3/4" hem.

5. Top-stitch hem along upper edge leaving an opening to insert elastic.

6. Insert elastic in casing/hem. Check for desired fit.

7. Lap elastic 1/2" and stitch to secure.

PULL ELASTIC TO DESIRED FIT

8. Finish hem top-stitching.

BOTTOM HEMS

1. Cut garment length 1 3/4" longer than desired finished length.

2. According to pattern directions, sew garment up to but not including the hem.

3. Turn up 1 3/4" hem.

4. Top-stitch hem along upper edge of hem.

5. Through one center front opening, insert a long length of elastic into the casing/hem.

6. Stitch to secure elastic at one center front edge.

7. Pull loose end of elastic to desired length.

8. Stitch to secure elastic at the other center front edge. Cut off excess elastic.

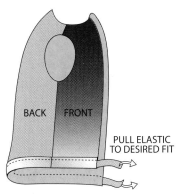

BACK FRONT

PULL ELASTIC TO DESIRED FIT

PART SIX

NO HASSLE ZIPPERS: AND SO MUCH MORE!

Everything you ever wanted to know about zippers (and some things you never even thought about!)

When you begin to study fleece garments in better ready-to-wear stores, you will discover that they carry pretty hefty price tags. Also, you will frequently notice special detailing or finishing techniques that set them above and apart from ordinary run-of-the-mill clothing.

This chapter begins with basic zipper applications. Then discover some clever famous label techniques and learn a few "cheater" methods!

NANCY'S HINT:

Before you even start, make your sewing life a whole lot easier and have a roll of 1/4" double-sided wash-away basting tape on hand. It is one of those little sewing notions that, as my grandmother used to say is "The best thing since sliced bread." When it comes to applying zippers, wash-away basting tape is worth its weight in gold and the "only way to go." My favorite is Collins Wash-A-Way Wondertape.

FIRST THINGS FIRST: TIRED OF TOO LONG ZIPPERS? SEWERS UNITE – WE DON'T HAVE TO FIGHT THEM ANYMORE!

Have you ever noticed?

The pattern calls for a 26" zipper...so you buy a 26" zipper. You cut and sew the garment without making any alterations. Yet, you end up one or two zipper teeth too long or too short!

Too short is unacceptable because there is a gap.

Too long used to be a hassle because of the bulk that resulted from folding the excess length out of the way.

But now, no more zipper hassle! Thanks go to Susan Pleas of Sutrumara for this clever idea. Use this easy shortening method and all your sport zippers will be "right on the money"!

NANCY'S HINT:

Since this method makes it easy to get the exact zipper length necessary, I always buy zippers at least 4" longer than I think I need. This gives me the freedom to alter my garment length in the middle of a project. I can take advantage of a perhaps more flattering design placement or add a design repeat without worrying whether my zipper will fit.

NANCY'S QUICK & EASY NO-BULK ZIPPER SHORTENING METHOD

(FOR MOLDED, PLASTIC-TOOTHED SPORT ZIPPERS)

Note: Always shorten zippers from the top end.

1. Buy the sport zipper longer than required. *Better safe than sorry!*

2. Sew the "too-long" zipper in place, up to the desired height.

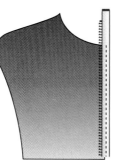

3. Back-tack to secure stitching.

4. Unzip the zipper.

5. Use Fiskar Diagonal Cutters to cut off approximately 1" of plastic teeth above the back-tack. Cut off only the plastic portion of the zipper tooth that extends beyond the zipper tape. Use the points of the cutters to "tweeze" the remaining plastic part that is adhered to the zipper tape. The result will be a smooth, empty section of zipper tape.

Remember: Do not zip up the zipper until it has been secured in a seamline or has the tape folded under to create a "stop." If you get too enthusiastic and zip up early, you will spend the next couple hours trying to get the @#!!* zipper pull back on. If that happens, this clever technique will have lost some of its charm!

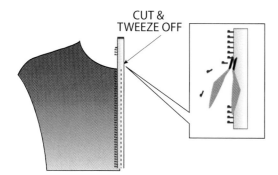

CUT &
TWEEZE OFF

6. Cut off excess zipper tape **above** the 1" of "toothless" section of tape. You need the toothless section for Step #7

7. To create your own "zipper stop," you may purchase separate stops, hand or machine bar-tack at the top edge of the last

tooth, catch tape in a seamline or fold the smooth "toothless" zipper tape back onto itself at a 45°.

Note: Since you are removing the original "real" zipper stop, before progressing with sewing, make sure that the bartack, fold-over, or seamline creates enough of a "new stop" to prevent the zipper pull from sliding off the end. This is not a typical problem, however, it is better to test now rather than work to correct it later!

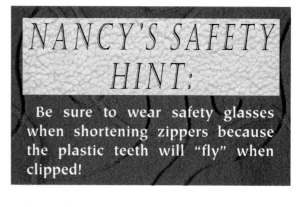

NANCY'S SAFETY HINT:

Be sure to wear safety glasses when shortening zippers because the plastic teeth will "fly" when clipped!

Fiskar Diagonal Cutters are .040 copper wire cutters with short pointed blades. I find they work the best. They are available at your favorite fabric or craft store. I tried "regular" wire cutters from my husband's workbench and found them too big to accurately cut off one tooth at a time and smaller cutters don't have the helpful built-in spring mechanism in the handle.

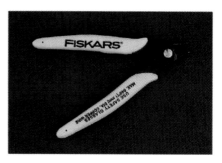

TO SHORTEN METAL ZIPPERS

Fiskar Diagonal Cutters are not strong enough to cut metal zipper teeth.

To shorten metal zippers, use two pairs of household pliers. Use one pair of pliers to grasp the zipper tape close to the base of the metal tooth. Be careful that the pliers are only grasping the cloth tape.

Use the other pair of pliers to grasp the tip of a metal tooth and pull. Take care that the pliers are only grasping a metal tip.

TO SHORTEN NYLON COIL ZIPPERS

1. Sew the "too-long" nylon coil zipper in place up to desired height.
2. Back-tack to secure stitching.
3. Trim zipper 3/4" above back-tack.
4. Fold excess zipper back onto itself at about a 45° angle and stitch in place.

TRADITIONAL ZIPPERS

Zippers can be applied "in the usual way" by following the pattern's sewing directions.

Great Tips Worth Trying

1. Rather than pin the zipper in place, use wash-away basting tape. Apply tape along outer edges of zipper tape and peel off paper backing. It is easy to tape zipper in place and you can easily see where you are stitching.
2. Avoid buckling zippers: When taping the zipper into place, work on a flat surface and be absolutely scrupulous about laying the

fleece with a 1:1 ratio onto the zipper tape. Never stretch or tug to make anything fit! The more gently it is handled and the more evenly the zipper is taped, the smoother the results.
3. Remember that a stretchy fleece is being sewn onto a rigid zipper tape. Use a longer stitch length and sew slowly to keep everything smooth. If the machine wants to "skootch" the fleece layer, experiment with decreasing the presser foot pressure.
4. If sewing on an ancient machine, or if constantly fighting the machine's feed system, instead of using the narrow zipper foot, try using the regular presser foot. Move the needle position to the far left or far right. The regular presser foot gives more contact with the feed dogs.

UNTRADITIONAL ZIPPERS: BLUNT EDGE METHOD

As discussed in Seam Options in Part 4, fleece doesn't ravel or fray and frequently the clean, blunt, cut edge of the fleece can be used to your advantage. Zipper insertion is one of these times.

If using a thick fleece that results in a nice blunt edge when cut, simply lay the blunt edge alongside the zipper teeth and top-stitch in place. This is especially nice on bulky fleece where a turned-under fleece seam allowance on the zipper tape would be cumbersome. It also reduces "buckle" on fleeces with more stretch because only one layer of fleece is being sewn.

1. Cut 1/4" off the seam allowance.
2. Apply wash-away basting tape on the **right** side of the zipper, along the outer edges of the zipper tape.
3. Lay the blunt cut edge of the fleece 1/8" to 1/4" away from the zipper teeth, adhering in place. It should be far enough away so that the fleece will not get caught in the zipper.

4. Top-stitch through fleece and zipper. *The Untraditional Zipper: Blunt Edge Method is not suitable for pile fabrics with a long pile that might get caught in the zipper teeth. If in doubt, test first.*

NAKED ZIPPERS: TRADITIONAL ZIPPERS WITHOUT FACINGS

When looking at garments in ready-to-wear, you will notice that they frequently bypass the step sandwiching the zipper between the garment and the facing. The facing is completely eliminated, which leaves an exposed (naked) zipper tape. Elimination of the facing greatly reduces the bulk factor. There are now only three layers (garment front, front seam allowance and zipper tape) as opposed to five layers (the above plus facing and facing seam allowance).

Have some fun and add a splash of color with the next technique "Dressing the Naked Zipper."

DRESSING THE NAKED ZIPPER

This technique is found on better brands such as Lands' End and Patagonia.

Today fleece garments are worn indoors as often as outdoors. Most of the major pattern companies feature close-fitting pullovers to wear indoors or as a first layer for cold outdoor activi-

ties. Many of these close-fitting garments feature zippers up the front and through the turtleneck. To reduce bulk, the facings are simply eliminated.

The elimination of front

facings successfully reduces bulk, but leaves an exposed "naked" zipper which tends to look unfinished and inexpensive. To "dress" naked zipper tapes, simply wrap the edges of the zipper tape before applying the zipper to your garment! This is quick, easy, classy and looks expensive!

When the neckline is worn open, the little bit of ribbon accent, dressing the zipper, looks terrific!

See "Added Bonus" for using this idea as a problem solver.

GROSGRAIN WRAPPED

Requirements
5/8" grosgrain ribbon – two times longer than the zipper length

Note: I prefer 5/8" grosgrain ribbon to dress my zippers. It is 100% polyester, comes in a wide range of colors and is easily found at both fabric and craft stores. However, any colorfast washable trim with finished edges will work.

Zipper – Use a nylon coil zipper for indoor or close-fitting garments because it is softer and more comfortable. Use a sport zipper for outerwear.

1. Press the ribbon in half, lengthwise. *Note: Some ribbons and trim are "springy" and not excited about being pressed in half. However, with extra steam, pressure and time, you will win. If you have an exceptionally stubborn piece of trim, use wash-away basting tape to adhere trim to the zipper tape. The tape does not gum up the needle and will wash away in the first laundering.*

2. Slip the folded ribbon over each long edge of the zipper tape. Encase the edges and edge-stitch in place. Use an edge-stitch presser foot for ease and accuracy.

3. Apply the zipper to the garment according to pattern directions.

When the neckline is worn open, the little bit of color accent, dressing the zipper, looks terrific!

ADDED BONUS: DRESSING NAKED ZIPPERS TO SOLVE COLOR PROBLEMS!

Dressing a naked zipper does a great job of getting you out of trouble when it is difficult to find coordinating zippers and ribbing.

Plan of Attack

Ribbing is always available to match a zipper. Zippers come in a relatively basic range of colors. Choose a zipper that will compliment the fabric and purchase ribbing to match the zipper.

Note: They do not need to match the fleece, just compliment it.

Then (here's the fun part) choose a totally different color of grosgrain ribbon to "dress" the zipper tape! This looks sharp, it's easy and it opens up a whole world of possibilities when you can't find "matching" colors!

ZIPPER INSERTION BEHIND WRAPPED EDGE FINISHES

When it comes time to sew the zipper into the garment, it can't be much easier.

1. If necessary, shorten the zipper according to the "No-Bulk" shortening technique on page 69.
2. Place wash-away basting tape on the outer edges of the zipper tape and tape in place behind the finished wrapped edge (**right** side of zipper against the **wrong** side of the garment).
3. At the upper edge, fold the excess zipper tape out of the way so it does not get caught in a seam. Tuck the excess tape, *between the zipper and the garment*, to the **wrong** side.

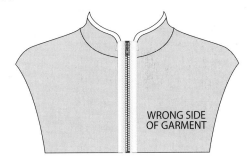

WRONG SIDE OF GARMENT

4. Edge-stitch on the trim strip next to the zipper teeth. Catch the zipper tape underneath.
5. Stitch on the outer edge of trim strip. If constructed "The Hard Way," stitch over the first stitching. If constructed "The Cheater's Way," this will be the only outer edge-stitching.

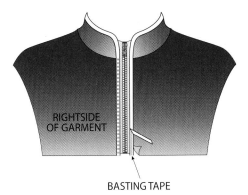

RIGHTSIDE OF GARMENT

BASTING TAPE

SUPER EASY ZIPPERED POCKETS

This zipper is most frequently seen on pull-overs and jackets. It is set at an angle and top-stitched over an inner pocket.

If you love the pattern you are making, but cringe at the complicated zippered pocket directions, try this no-fail method for easy zippered pockets.

NANCY'S HINT:

Whenever drawing lines onto stay material for pockets, tab fronts or any other pattern tracing requirements use a #1 soft lead pencil. Avoid ballpoint pens or felt markers, as they can later smudge ink onto the fabric and may be difficult to remove.

1. For the pocket stay, use tear-away stabilizer or pattern tracing material. Draw a rectangle 4" wide by 4" longer than the zipper length. For example: If the pattern requires a 7" zipper, then the stay will be 4" wide by 11" long.

2. Create a stitching line by drawing a rectangle, centered in the stay, 1/2" wide by the exact length of the zipper teeth, from zipper stop to zipper stop.

3. Create a cutting line by drawing a center line and 1/2" high wedges at each short end of the box.

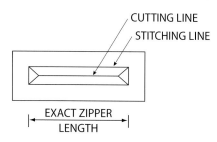

CUTTING LINE
STITCHING LINE
EXACT ZIPPER LENGTH

4. Match the pattern's placement marks and pin the stay to the right side of the garment.

5. Use a shorter stitch length for extra strength and sew around the box. Begin and end stitching on one long side of the box. Overlap the stitches at the starting point.

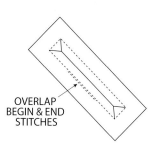

OVERLAP BEGIN & END STITCHES

NANCY'S HINT:

Perfectly matched short box ends - As you pivot to stitch the first short end, count the number of stitches you take. When you reach the other short end sew the same exact number of stitches, regardless of the drawn lines. Can't help but be even!

6. Use sharp scissors to cut on the center cutting line. Cut into the corners of the wedge through the stay and the fleece, being careful not to cut through the stitching.

7. Turn the stay to the **wrong** side, through the cut-open box, to finished position.

STEP 5 – RIGHT SIDE

STEP 5 – WRONG SIDE

STEP 7 – WRONG SIDE

STEP 7 – RIGHT SIDE

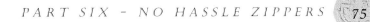

8. From the **wrong** side of the garment, gently steam and finger press while rolling seams to the underside. Do not touch the iron to the fleece.

BASTING TAPE

9. Apply wash-away basting tape to the outer edges of the **right** side of the zipper tape.

10. Place the closed zipper behind each box opening and finger press to adhere. Check to make sure that the zipper pull is at the desired end of the box and that the stay material is not visible from the right side of the garment.

11. Edge-stitch around the box, catching the zipper tape in the stitching. Begin and end on one long side.

12. Top-stitch 1/4", around the entire box, catching the zipper tape in the stitching. Begin and end on one long side.

13. On the inside of the garment, trim stay close to stitching and discard.

14. Choose one of the following methods to complete the backside of pockets:

A. If the jacket has a separate upper yoke and lower front, cut two lower fronts for each side. After zippered pocket is complete, baste the two lower fronts together. The back layer creates one large pocket.

B. If the jacket has a separate upper yoke and lower front, cut a separate "panel" to lay behind the pocket. Top-stitch in place to create a moderate-sized pocket.

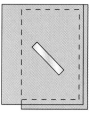

C. Pocket Shapes - From the same fabric as the garment front, cut out a pocket shape (rectangle, oblong, square, irregular geometric) and place it on the **wrong** side of the front, behind the pocket opening. From the **wrong** side of the garment, top-stitch in place. *Note: This is perfect for garments without yokes, garments without side seams or when a top-stitched pocket shape will add interest to an otherwise plain garment front.*

CUT AND SEW POCKET

This is similar to the Super Easy Zippered Pocket, only quicker and easier! It is yet another example of how to take advantage of the no-ravel, no-fray characteristics of fleece.

1. Use a fabric pencil to draw an opening for a zippered pocket directly onto the garment front. Draw a box 1/2" wide by the exact length of the zipper teeth, from zipper stop to zipper stop.

2. Cut the box opening. (Be exact since this will be the visible blunt cut edge sewn next to the zipper teeth.) For a fun look on a child's garment, cut opening using pinking shears.

3. Apply wash-away basting tape along the outer edges of the **right** side of zipper tape.

4. Place the closed zipper, behind the box opening, and finger press to adhere. (Double check to make sure that the zipper pull is at

the desired end of the box.)

5. Edge-stitch around the box, beginning and ending on one long side while catching the zipper tape in the stitching.

6. Top-stitch at 1/4", around the entire box, beginning and ending on one long side while catching the zipper tape in the stitching.

7. Complete backside of pocket per A., B., or C. above.

TWO-FROM-ONE POCKET ZIPPER TRICK

Buying Sport Zippers can frequently be a frustrating experience. When you need one long zipper for a jacket front and two short zippers for the pockets, the stores always seem to only have two out of three! Even if only two zippers are required for a pair of pockets, then the store only has one!?! Is this a conspiracy?

Use the clever "Quick 'N Easy No-Bulk Zipper Shortening" technique, discussed on page 69, and take one long, dual separating zipper and convert it into two pocket length zippers!

Follow directions for the "Super Easy Zippered Pockets" to draw pocket stay and install zippers.

1. Choose a dual separating zipper that is at least twice the length of one pocket zipper (because you are doing two pockets), plus 5" to 6" extra zipper length.

2. Make sure that both zipper pulls are identical so that the pocket zippers match!

3. Cut the zipper in half to create two half zippers.

Note: Before cutting apart, make sure that the zipper is closed with one zipper pull at each end. This way you will have two closed half-zippers, each with a zipper pull.

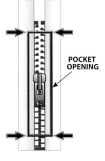

POCKET OPENING

4. Move each zipper pull to the center of each half zipper.

5. Place each half-zipper behind the zippered pocket openings and mark the last zipper tooth for each end.

6. To create closed zipper ends, machine or hand bar-tack after each marked tooth.

7. Use Fiskar Diagonal Cutters to trim plastic teeth 1" beyond each bar-tack.

8. Trim excess zipper tape leaving 3/4" beyond each bar-tack.

9. Apply wash-away basting tape and sew the zipper into the box opening.

This technique is also great for those times when perhaps you are not the most precise sewing person in the world. No one will be any the wiser.

If one box opening happens to be 6 7/8" long, while the other box happens to be 7 1/4" long, it will not make a difference. You will be cutting each zipper length to fit each box opening.

You wouldn't be so lucky using purchased 7" zippers, your less-than-precise sewing would not be so secret. Buckling would have occurred on one pocket and gapping on the other.

"BACKWARDS" ZIPPER
(WITH HIDDEN SEAM ALLOWANCES)

I was shopping in an upscale sportswear shop when I saw this clever technique. The seams along the zipper, the hood edge, the roll-up cuffs and the top edge of the pockets were finished the same way. The result was a clean, smooth edge that was completely finished inside and out!

First, the zipper application will be discussed. Ideas to coordinate pockets, hoods, and cuffs will follow.

I call this the "Backwards Zipper" because it is sewn backwards! The zipper is sewn to the ***wrong*** *side of the garment. The zipper tape and the seam allowance are then turned to the* ***right*** *side of the garment! The seam allowance and zipper tape are "hidden" underneath a decorative trim for both a functional and fashionable finish.*

NC's IMPORTANT NOTE: Since there will be no front facings, it is important that the neck finish (hood, ribbing or collar) ends flush with the center front edge. The "Backwards Zipper" application is not suitable for collars that are set back from the front edge requiring a facing to finish the upper edge, like a lapel point

Color Options

Many options are available. You are no longer restricted to "matching" colors.

Use purchased pre-decorated ribbon trim, plain ribbon trim and add decorative stitching or UltraSuede strips with embellishing stitches.

Choose the ribbon color to match a contrasting zipper. Use decorative stitches that match fleece color.

Choose the zipper to match the fabric and use a contrasting ribbon color. Use decorative stitches that match fleece color.

Choose a contrasting zipper and a second contrasting color for the ribbon. Use decorative stitches that match zipper color.

Substitute UltraSuede strips for grosgrain ribbon and use any of the options above.

Requirements

5/8" grosgrain ribbon - measure all the edges to be finished and add extra for experimental sample stitching

Or, UltraSuede 4" x 45" cut to 5/8" strips

Decorative thread for embellishing stitches on trim

Thread to match grosgrain ribbon or **UltraSuede trim** for edge-stitching in place

Tear-away stabilizer - 1 yard

Wash-A-Way Wonder Tape

Note: During the various stages of construction, as necessary, change the needle and bobbin thread to match the fabric or trim.

Throughout directions, all trims are referred to as "ribbon."

EMBELLISH STITCHING THE RIBBON

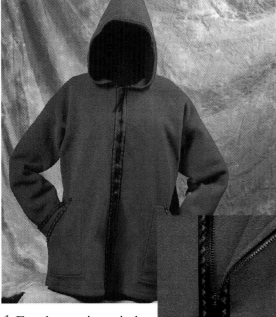

1. For decorative stitching, cut tear-away stabilizer into approximately 1" wide strips and slip underneath the ribbon to stabilize. Choose a

decorative stitch, or sequence of stitches on the machine. With decorative thread in the needle and regular thread in the bobbin, decorative stitch the entire length of the ribbon. Replace strips of stabilizer as necessary.

For more visible decorative stitching, choose decorative stitches with a fair amount of satin stitching detail.

2. Tear away stabilizer and discard.
3. Press ribbon flat.

"BACKWARDS ZIPPER" APPLICATION

Since this is an unusual zipper application, please read through the directions before you begin to sew. Pay careful attention to **right** and **wrong** sides of garment and zipper. The end result is a lovely finished inside edge with no visible seam allowances or zipper tape. The seam allowances and zipper tape are "hidden" underneath the decorative ribbon!

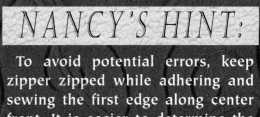

NANCY'S HINT:

To avoid potential errors, keep zipper zipped while adhering and sewing the first edge along center front. It is easier to determine the *wrong* side of the zipper when it is zipped! Do not unzip the zipper until it has been adhered to the second side and is ready to be stitched.

IMPORTANT NOTES:

The following directions are for zipper application only. Refer to the pattern directions for the order of sewing and the finishing details regarding the neck and bottom finish.

Before beginning, completely read through your pattern's directions, "Backwards" Zipper directions and the Neckline Guidelines to determine the best approach for a particular garment.
1. Eliminate front facings, if necessary.
2. Apply wash-away basting tape to the **wrong** side of the zipper, along the outer edges of the zipper tape.
3. **Wrong** sides together, use the basting

tape to adhere the zipper to one side of the garment front. Place zipper tape even with the raw edge of center front, zipper teeth pointing away from center front (towards body). *Note: This is not the normal way of applying a zipper.*

4. Place upper and lower ends of zipper according to the pattern directions. At the top edge, fold excess zipper tape or zipper length out of the way. If necessary to shorten the sport zipper, see "Quick 'N Easy No-Bulk Zipper Shortening Method" on page 69. Remove zipper teeth from the excess area, but do not trim excess zipper tape yet.

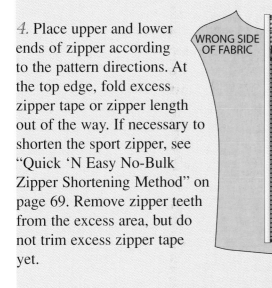

WRONG SIDE OF FABRIC

¼"

5. Stitch zipper to one side of the garment using 1/4" seam allowance.

6. Adhere zipper to the other side of center front. Unzip and stitch.

7. Turn zipper to finished position and double check to make sure the zipper teeth point away from body and the zipper tape and seam allowance are on the **right** side of the garment. Also, make sure the inside is smooth, with a finished seamline.

8. Beginning at **bottom left side of center front** (as when wearing), place decoratively stitched ribbon alongside, and 1/8" away from, the zipper teeth. Leave 1/2" ribbon extending below the bottom

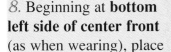

RIGHT SIDE OF FABRIC

edge (in case you need it to wrap or finish the lower edge, depending upon your pattern's bottom edge finish).

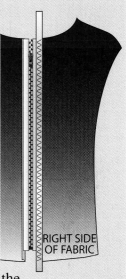

9. Begin at the lower edge and edge-stitch ribbon to the zipper tape. This is the side of the ribbon closest to the zipper teeth. Be careful not to catch any fleece on the underside.

RIGHT SIDE OF FABRIC

10. Trim any excess zipper tape that was folded out of the way at the neckline. Leave only an amount that will be entirely covered by the ribbon. *Note: This step may not apply to your particular pattern.*

11. Alongside the un-stitched edge, apply wash-away basting tape to the **wrong** side of the entire length of the ribbon. Adhere ribbon in place.

12. Edge-stitch, sewing through the ribbon and the fleece, completely enclosing the zipper tape and seam allowance.

13. Finish lower edge of garment according to pattern directions.

NECK SEAM FINISH

A nice finishing touch is to hide the inside neck seam under embellished ribbon.

1. Sew neckline seam using a conventional sewing machine. Finger press seam allowance open.
2. Cut a piece of ribbon 1" longer than the sewn neck seam.
3. Apply basting tape to the **wrong** side of the cut ribbon, centering it down the entire length of the ribbon.
4. Completely covering seam allowance raw edges on the inside of the garment, adhere ribbon over the finger-pressed-open neck seam allowance.
5. At center front edges, tuck ribbon under to create finished edges.
6. Edge-stitch along both sides of the ribbon. Experiment using a edge-stitch presser foot and a zipper presser foot to determine which works best on your machine.
7. At center front, whip-stitch the edges of the ribbon to the front edge.

NECKLINE GUIDELINES: HOW TO HANDLE DIFFERENT NECKLINE STYLES

REGULAR COLLAR OR BASEBALL STYLE RIBBING

If neck has a regular collar or baseball style ribbing, the zipper embellished ribbon will end in the neck seamline.

1. Apply "Backwards Zipper" and ribbon trim.
2. Sew ribbing or collar to the neck edge. Catch the end of the embellished ribbon in the neck seam.
3. Finish inner neck seam with ribbon, if desired, according to above instructions.

ZIPPER THROUGH THE COLLAR STYLE

If neck finish is a zipper-through-the-collar style, the zipper embellished ribbon will be tucked under and whip-stitched at the upper edge of the collar.

1. Sew the single layer, outer collar, to the neck edge.
2. Apply "Backwards Zipper" to center front, ending zipper at the foldline of collar. Fold excess zipper tape out of the way.
3. Apply ribbon trim. Continue past the top end of the zipper to the end of the inner collar, turning under the center front edge of the inner collar.
4. **Wrong** sides together, fold the collar into finished position and whip-stitch finish the center front edge.
5. To finish, stitch the inner collar to the neck seam.

NECK EDGE FINISHED WITH A HOOD

If your neck edge is to be finished with a hood:

1. Sew hood to neckline.
2. Finish inner neck seam with ribbon, if desired, according to above instructions. Do not turn under ribbon at the center front edge.
3. Apply "Backwards Zipper."
4. When applying ribbon trim, continue past top of zipper around the hood edge.
5. When applying ribbon to the hood edge, fold 3/8" to the **right** side of garment. Lay ribbon on top along the folded hood edge and edge-stitch in place. The ribbon is applied in one continuous strip up one side of the center front, around the hood and down the other side.

"BACKWARDS PATCH POCKETS" – TO COORDINATE WITH THE "BACKWARDS ZIPPER"

Use stitch embellished ribbon to finish the upper edge of blunt-edged patch pockets.

1. Along the upper edge of the pocket, fold 3/8" to the **right** side of fabric.

2. Lay embellished ribbon along the fold. Leave 1/2" excess ribbon at each end.

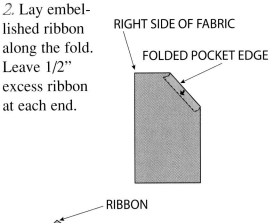

RIGHT SIDE OF FABRIC

FOLDED POCKET EDGE

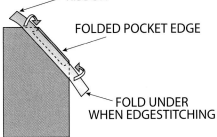

RIBBON

FOLDED POCKET EDGE

FOLD UNDER WHEN EDGESTITCHING

3. Edge-stitch ribbon along the side closest to the fold.

4. Apply wash-away basting tape to the other long side of ribbon.

5. Folding under the extra ribbon at the pocket sides, adhere ribbon in place.

6. Edge-stitch second side of ribbon in place.

7. Apply basting tape to outer edges on the **wrong** side of the pocket. Adhere the pocket to the garment.

8. Edge-stitch outer pocket edges. Then top-stitch 1/4" away from edge-stitching.

"BACKWARDS ROLL-UP CUFFS" – TO COORDINATE WITH THE "BACKWARDS ZIPPER"

Use stitch embellished ribbon to finish the upper edge of roll-up cuffs.

This technique is suitable for fabrics without an obvious wrong side.

1. Cut sleeves 3" longer than desired finished length.

2. **Right** sides together, sew sleeve from underarm point stopping 3" from the bottom edge of the sleeve.

3. Lay the **wrong** side of embellished ribbon on the **right** side of the sleeve hem edge. Extend ribbon 3/8" beyond sleeve hem raw edge.

4. Edge-stitch in place.

5. Apply basting tape on the wrong side of the unsewn edge of ribbon.

6. Turn ribbon to the **wrong** side of sleeve and adhere in place.

7. Edge-stitch second side of ribbon.

RIGHT SIDE OF SLEEVE

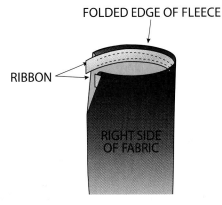

FOLDED EDGE OF FLEECE

RIBBON

RIGHT SIDE OF FABRIC

8. **Wrong** sides together, finish sewing lower part of sleeve.

9. Roll up 3" cuff to finished position.

PART SEVEN

BUTTONHOLES ON FLEECE: CHALLENGES & SOLUTIONS

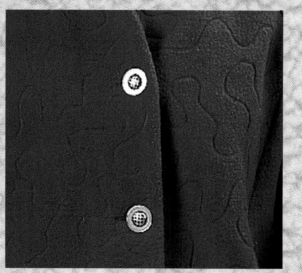

Ready-to-wear garments rely on zippers rather than buttonholes. Fleece garments lack the stability necessary for rough and tumble buttonholes because they rarely incorporate interfacing.

This chapter addresses the times when only buttonholes will suffice.

Buttonholes on fleece and pile fabrics, while not difficult, do present some challenges that require different approaches.

THE GOLDEN RULE OF BUTTONHOLES

Before making buttonholes on the actual garment, always sew practice samples to exactly duplicate the conditions. Make sure everything is the same; grain, thread, stabilizers, stitch length, etc.

CHALLENGE #1

Because fleeces have a fuzzy and sometimes bumpy surface, it is difficult to mark visible and accurate buttonholes.

SOLUTION

Draw the buttonholes onto pieces of a Sulky Solvy (water-soluble stabilizer) and pin in place. Or, draw onto Stick-dSolv (adhesive water soluble stabilizer) and adhere in place. Stitch the buttonhole. Rinse to dissolve stabilizer when finished.

Important Note: When drawing buttonholes onto water soluble stabilizers, be sure to use a permanent marker, a wash-out marker or a disappearing ink marker. You want to be sure that there is no staining when the stabilizer is rinsed away. I like to use an ink color compatible with my thread color. If some stabilizer remains for a laundering or two, it doesn't really show.

CHALLENGE #2

Fleece is spongy and lofty, causing the buttonhole stitches to sink in.

SOLUTION

The Solution to Challenge #1 also solves this problem. Solvy or Stick-dSolv will help keep the stitches laying on top of the fabric rather than sinking in. Also, slipping a layer of tear-away stabilizer underneath the buttonhole will help maintain the stitch integrity on the backside of the buttonhole.

CHALLENGE #3

Avoid the dreaded "frogmouth!"

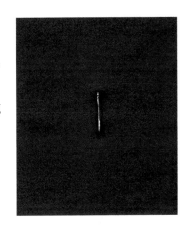

"Frogmouth" is a wavy, gaping opening when the buttonhole is cut open.

The primary cause, of the dreaded "frogmouth," is that the stitch density is too tight. Because fleece is a stretch knit, if too much thread is piled in, the buttonhole edges will "ruffle" as soon as the buttonhole opening is cut.

SOLUTION #1

Loosen the satin stitch density (stitch length) from the preset setting on the machine. Loosen the stitch so that a little bit of fabric is visible between the stitches.

SOLUTION #2

Follow the directions in the sewing machine manual for making a corded button-hole. When finished, draw up the cording to the desired length. Use a hand sewing needle with a large eye to pull the cording thread tails to the wrong side. Tie in a knot to secure and cut the ends.

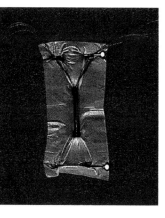

SOLUTION #3

Solutions to Challenges #1 and #2, using water-soluble stabilizer on the top and tear-away stabilizer underneath will also help prevent the dreaded "frog-mouth."

SOLUTION #4

If the fleece is sturdy and not too stretchy, sew a simple straight stitch box for the buttonhole. Use a shorter straight-stitch length, 2.5mm or 12 stitches per inch, rather than the tradi-tional zigzag stitch buttonhole box.

To insure even box ends, count the stitches on the first box end and then do the same number of stitches on the other end!

NANCY'S HINT:

There is no need to purchase cording to match your fabric...you already have it! Simply use a long strand of sewing machine thread (which already matches your fabric). Fold the strand in half. Then fold in half again creating four strands of thread. Use the four strands "as one" to cord the buttonhole. This is quick, strong and a perfect match.

CHALLENGE #4: INTERFACING BUTTONHOLES

Since interfacing is rarely used in fleece garments, the usual source of stabilization for buttonholes does not exist.

SOLUTION

If there are two layers of fleece fabric (separate facings, cuffs or collar), slip a 2" or 3" square of non-stretch interfacing between the fabric layers in the buttonhole area. Then sew buttonholes, incorporating some of the above solutions.

NANCY'S HINT:

When sewing the buttons in place, add a little extra strength and avoid potential "pull-through" by sewing a small flat button on the wrong side, behind the fashion button. This is especially important for those times when the buttons will be sewn onto a single layer of fleece.

TOO GOOD TO BE TRUE BUTTONHOLE

Thanks go out to Pat Headen of Hartsdale Fabrics in New York for this clever, and "much too easy" buttonhole idea.

The basis is simple: Use self fabric to stabilize the buttonhole! This is perfect to use on single layer garments when interfacing is not an option.

1. **Wrong** sides together, place a patch of self fabric behind each buttonhole area. Don't be too particular about the shape or size because the patch will be cut away when finished.
2. Place the patch so that the greater degree of stretch in the patch is opposite the greater degree of stretch in the garment.

3. Sew the buttonhole. Sew a traditional loose zigzag stitch or a straight stitch box type as discussed in Challenge #3, Solution #4.
4. Use sharp scissors to trim patch away. Trim very close to the buttonhole stitching.

The resultant double layer of fabric in the buttonhole stitching provides just the right amount of extra stabilization necessary. Because self fabric is used, the color match is perfect!

Suggestion: Before making your final buttonhole decision read on for Sport Snap information as an alternative. Also, see Part 8: A Touch of Class - UltraSuede Accents to find options such as UltraSuede button loops and UltraSuede buttonhole patches.

Sport snaps offer an excellent alternative to buttons and buttonholes. I have tested a variety of brands and highly recommend the snaps from *The Snap Source*. They have long prongs which easily accommodate the loft of fleece and remain secure. *Snap Source* snaps are the same as those used in ready-to-wear and the color range is quite extensive.

There are two basic sport snap styles: post-style and prong-style.

The post-style snaps require a hole in the fabric enabling the snap to attach to the fabric. These are designed for use with woven fabrics.

Prong-style snaps attach to the fabric by self-piercing. Prong-style is the proper choice for knits. When purchasing sport snaps, be careful to get prong-style snaps as fleece and pile fabrics are knits.

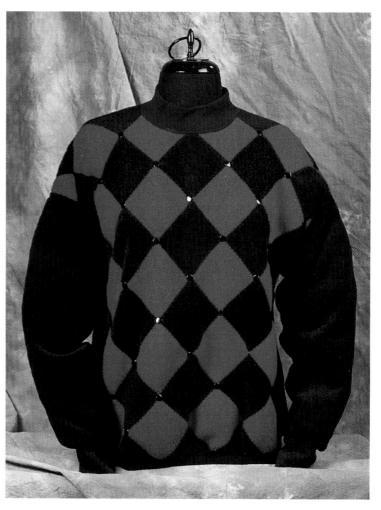

Jeanine Twigg, founder and owner of The Snap Source (and author of the book *It's a Snap!*), provided excellent information for snap application to fleece.

Snaps come in a variety of sizes from baby small to jumbo heavy duty.

Size 20 (1/2") or larger is preferable for polar type fabrics. **The Snap Setter** attaching tool makes snap application

quick and simple. Snap application to fleeces is easy. The longer prongs handle up to two layers of 200 or mid-weight fleece, including the necessary

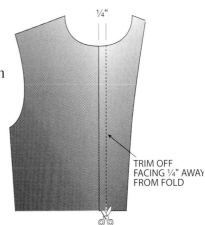

2. If the garment has a fold back cut-on facing, trim the facing to 1/4" beyond the front foldline.

¼"

TRIM OFF FACING ¼" AWAY FROM FOLD

3. Retrace the cut-away facing, adding 1/2" to the front "cut" edge or simply draw a completely new facing 2" wide x center front length.

ADD ½"

CUT FROM WOVEN FABRIC

interfacing. However, if you are dealing with a heavy, dense, bulky fleece or if you don't want the bulk of interfaced

double layers overlapped at center front, use Jeanine's bulk-reducing method.

JEANINE'S "BULKLESS" FACING

1. Choose a complimentary lighter weight woven fabric for the facing. These types of fabric include cotton prints, nylon Supplex, lightweight denim, etc.

4. Cut two new front facings from woven fabric.
5. Interface the new facings.
6. **Right** sides together, sew interfaced woven facing to the fleece garment along the center front. Use a 1/4" seam allowance.
7. Finish remaining edge of facing as desired.
8. Turn facing to finished position and top-stitch.
9. Apply **Sport Snaps** following manufacturer's directions.

Replacing the thicker fleece facing with a lighter layer of fabric automatically reduces the bulk at the closure area while allowing the snaps to penetrate the fabric easier. The interfaced woven fabric also adds stability.

PART EIGHT

A TOUCH OF CLASS: ULTRASUEDE ACCENTS

UltraSuede can be used for a fashion statement or for pure practicality. It compliments polars, Berbers and everything in between! These ideas are designed for regular weight UltraSuede and other comparable suede products. UltraSuede Light, formerly known as Facile is too lightweight for these applications.

ULTRASUEDE DRAWCORD OR HOOD TIE

When the garment requires a drawcord finish or hood tie, UltraSuede offers a wide range of lush rich colors to compliment any fabric. A cotton drawcord looks dull against rich fleece colors and polyester drawcord has a limited range of available color choices.

Requirements
UltraSuede - one 2" x 45" strip
Fusible Web
Thread - coordinating

1. Following manufacturer's directions, iron fusible web to the **wrong** side of UltraSuede. Do not place the iron in direct contact with UltraSuede. Use a press cloth.

2. Cut UltraSuede strip into two 1" x 45" strips.

3. Peel off paper backing from fusible web.

4. Overlap UltraSuede strips at one short end and stitch together to form one long 1" x 90" strip.

5. Fold UltraSuede strip in half, lengthwise to 1/2" x 90" and press to adhere.

6. Trim strips to 3/8". Leave folded edge intact and neaten by trimming raw edges.

7. Edge-stitch along both long sides of UltraSuede drawcord.

BUTTONHOLE LOOPS: FOR MODERATE USE

Requirements
UltraSuede - one 1" x 45" strip will make approximately seven buttonhole loops
Fusible Web
Thread - coordinating

1. Follow UltraSuede Drawcord directions, steps #1-3, #5-7.

2. Cut long drawcord into 6" strips for loops. Before cutting, check to make sure this is long enough to accommodate the button size.

3. Follow the pattern directions for button-hole placement. Arrange Buttonhole Loops according to diagram and stitch to secure. Make sure the Buttonhole Loop is large enough to fit over the button, yet snug enough not to easily come unbuttoned.

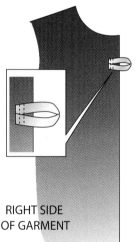

RIGHT SIDE OF GARMENT

BUTTONHOLE TABS: FOR LIGHTWEIGHT USE

Requirements
UltraSuede - 1" x 45" will create approximately ten Buttonhole Tabs
Thread - coordinating

1. For each tab, cut **single** layer strips of UltraSuede 1/2" x 9".

2. Mark midpoint on the **wrong** side of each strip.

3. As illustrated, fold each end of the strip, **wrong** sides together, to form a pointed tab.

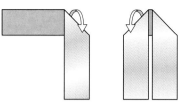

4. Stitch across the bottom of point to secure.

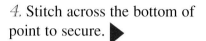

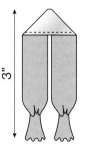

3"

5. Knot the ends of each strip so that the total tab measures 3" or whatever measurement is required for the garment and chosen button size.

6. Trim excess strip.

7. Follow the pattern directions for buttonhole placement. Arrange Buttonhole Tabs according to the diagram and stitch a box to secure. Buttonhole Tab should be large enough to fit over the button, yet snug enough not to easily come unbuttoned.

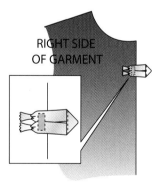

RIGHT SIDE OF GARMENT

BUTTONHOLE PATCHES: FOR HEAVY USE

Requirements
UltraSuede - one 2" x 45" strip
Thread - coordinating

1. Cut 2" squares, triangles, rectangles, or irregular geometric shapes as desired.

2. Follow the pattern directions for buttonhole placement and arrange Buttonhole Patches according to diagram and edge-stitch around patch to secure to garment front.

3. Center buttonholes in the patches and sew through the UltraSuede and the fleece.

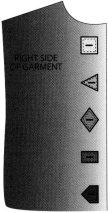

BUTTONHOLE PATCHES WITH LOOPS: FOR HEAVY USE

This technique gives a double dose of UltraSuede Patches, inside and outside, with extended Button Loops for heavy duty strength.

Requirements
UltraSuede - one 3" x 45" strip
Thread - coordinating
Wash-away Basting Tape

1. Use a 1" x 45" strip of UltraSuede and follow the "UltraSuede Drawcord" directions, steps #1-3, #5-7.
2. Cut long drawcord into 6" strips for loops. Make sure this is long enough for the button size.
3. Cut patches into 2" squares, triangles, rectangles, or irregular geometric shapes as desired.
4. Follow the pattern directions for buttonhole placement. Arrange buttonhole loops according to diagram and stitch to secure. Make sure the buttonhole loop is large enough to fit over the button, yet snug enough not to easily come unbuttoned.
5. Arrange buttonhole patches according to the diagram. Carefully aligning to match on the inside and the outside. Use wash-away basting tape all small letters or Fuse 'n Stick to adhere in place.
6. Top-stitch around outer edges of patch, sandwiching the buttonhole loops and catching the inside patch in the stitching.

ULTRA-EASY ULTRASUEDE ZIPPERED POCKETS

This is a combination of an UltraSuede patch and a zippered pocket. It is super quick and easy since all the UltraSuede edges are blunt cut raw edges. It offers a nice fashion accent rather than a heavy duty pocket.

Requirements

UltraSuede - two 9" x 9", or 6" x 9" pieces

Plastic-Toothed Sport Zippers - two 5" to 7"

Wash-away Basting Tape

1. Choose a pocket shape; square, rectangle, oblong or uneven geometric. The width of the pocket should be at least 2" wider than the zipper to be inserted.

2. Draw a box opening for the zipper, 3/8" wide by the length of the zipper teeth. *Note: measure from zipper stop to zipper stop.*

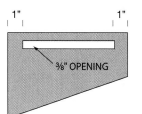

3. Cut on drawn box lines to create an opening for the zipper.

4. On the **right** side of the zipper, place wash-away basting tape along both outer edges of zipper tape.

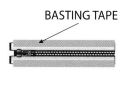

BASTING TAPE

5. Peel away protective paper and place zipper behind box. Finger press to adhere.

6. Use an edge-stitch presser foot to edge-stitch around the raw edges of the box opening, securing the zipper to the UltraSuede pocket.

7. Place wash-away basting tape on the **wrong** side of the UltraSuede Zippered Pocket, along the outer edge.

8. Place the pocket on the garment front as desired and finger press to adhere.

9. Edge-stitch pocket in place.

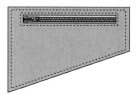

ULTRASUEDE ZIPPER PULLS

This is a small, but classy touch.

1. Cut a strip of UltraSuede 1/4" wide x 7" long.

2. Fold in half.

3. From the top, insert loop through the zipper pull opening.

4. Thread the tails through the loop and tighten knot.

5. Trim ends at an angle to the desired length.

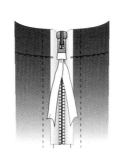

ULTRASUEDE ZIPPER TAB

This is a nice zipper ending and an even better "cover-up" when you are not happy with the appearance of the zipper end. This idea can be used when zippers end in a seam, in garments featuring zippers without seams and for pocket zippers that aren't up to your standards.

1. Cut a 1 1/2" triangle from UltraSuede.

2. Lay the triangle tab over the bottom of the zipper box. Edge-stitch lower angled sides.

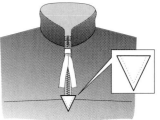

ULTRASUEDE POCKET FLAPS

The pocket flap is simply a layer of UltraSuede laid on top of the "Super Easy Zippered Pocket" in Part 6. This is used when you don't want the zipper to show. It also serves as a good "cover-up" if the zipper isn't quite the color you desire or if you just want to add a fun accent.

1. Choose a simple rectangle, a rectangle with pointed lower edge or a shape that echoes some other design aspect in the garment

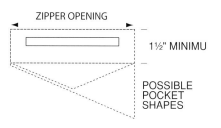

ZIPPER OPENING

1½" MINIMU

POSSIBLE POCKET SHAPES

and draw a pocket flap 1 1/2" longer than the finished zipper opening. It extends 3/4" beyond each end of the openings. Pocket flap and should be a minimum of 1 1/2" high, but depending on the shape, can be as deep as you desire.

2. Completely finish the zipper opening on the garment. **Do not** apply pocket backing or under pocket at this time.

3. Before placing pocket flap on garment, edge-stitch the upper edge of the pocket flap at 1/8" and top-stitch at 1/4".

4. Scotch tape pocket flap over pocket zipper. Extend flap 3/4" beyond each end of the zipper and just cover the upper edge of the zipper opening.

5. Edge-stitch and top-stitch the pocket flap to the garment, stitching around the sides and lower edges of the flap.

6. Finish inside pocket per directions for "Super Easy Zippered Pocket" in Part 6.

ULTRASUEDE YOKES

If the garment is just a little too plain for your taste and needs a little something to spark it up, add an UltraSuede yoke for a change of pace.

1. Overlay the commercial pattern piece for the front with a piece of pattern tracing material. Draw a yoke pattern piece by tracing center front, neckline, shoulder edge and armscye according to pattern. Trace the lower edge of the yoke making it as large and dramatic or as subtle as desired.

2. Cut out UltraSuede yokes.

3. Place the **wrong** side of UltraSuede yokes against **right** side of garment fronts.

4. Baste UltraSuede yokes to fronts at center front, neck edge, shoulder edge and armscye.

5. On lower edge of yokes, edge-stitch at 1/8", then top-stitch at 1/4".

6. If desired, stitch quilting lines or add decorative stitching lines.

7. Continue sewing garment according to pattern directions. Treat the yoke overlay and garment front as one.

8. If desired, repeat for the back. Trace yoke on the fold for one whole back yoke.

ULTRASUEDE PIPING

This is a fun and easy way to accent or sharply define a seamline. If you have a flair for the unusual, use a wavy or pinking blade on the rotary cutter for a shaped piping edge. Note: The piping in the pictured garment was cut with the wavy blade.

UltraSuede piping is suitable for insertion into straight or slightly curved seams.

1. Use a rotary cutter with a decorative or straight edge to cut strips of UltraSuede 3/8" wide if using a 1/4" seam allowance, or 3/4" wide if using a 5/8" seam allowance, by the width of the UltraSuede (45").

2. With the **wrong** side of UltraSuede strip against the **right** side of garment, place straight-edge of the piping strip against the raw edge of garment seam. Baste on 1/4" or 5/8" seamline. (Before basting, make certain that the piping will be in the desired finished position.)

3. Place garment **right** sides together, sandwiching the UltraSuede piping between the fabric layers.

4. Sew the seam, using the basting stitch line as a guide.

5. Finger press seam allowance away from the piping and top-stitch, if desired.

PART NINE

DESIGNER DETAILS

There is more to "designer details" than just changing collars, moving seamlines and altering sleeve styles. Fleeces and Berbers offer the creative machine artist a whole new canvas on which to work!

SCULPTURING FLEECE

This is probably the most fun and easy embellishing technique you can do!

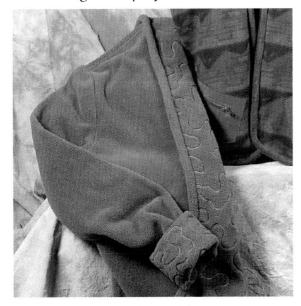

Sculpturing, also referred to as etching or engraving, gives a rich depth to the fleece. Satin stitching a continuous design, a

motif, outlining a print or simply meandering results in a dramatic grooved effect. This dramatic detailing can be used to "dress up" Polarfleece, lend a tone-on-tone effect to a one-color jacket or give a quilted effect when outlining a print. This type of detailing is equally effective on solids as well as prints, and dynamic on solid Berbers and shear-lings.

Sculpture

• the collar, fronts and cuffs of a jacket.
   • the shawl collar and pocket of a jacket.
   • down one side of a vest.
   • yokes or inset panels.
   • block (instead of color-block) a pull-over by dividing the front into a "tic-tac-toe" grid and sculpture in every other square.

The possibilities are unlimited.

Read through all the directions and ideas before beginning. There are hints, helps and things to consider sprinkled throughout the information.

Pattern - Choose a pattern that will be complimented with a "contrast" sculptured yoke, sleeve, pockets, cuff, inset, lapels, etc. *Sculpturing can be done anyplace where the backside of the sculpturing will never show.*
This qualification is necessary because the tear-away stabilizer remains visible.

Fabric - Most effective on fleece or Berber fabrics. *Note: Sculpturing does not show well on plushes.*

Needle Threads - Two or more spools. *Following is a listing of a variety of threads, the effects that they create and important information.*

Regular Thread – Gives shadowed "grooves."

Rayon Thread – Lends a lovely sheen to the "grooves."

Metallic Thread – Choose high quality thread. Sew slowly. Choose embroidery or metallic needle. Use needle lubricant.

Variegated Thread – Creates interesting effects.

Clear or Smoke Thread – Choose when outline sculpturing for a quilted effect. Perfect on a multi-colored print with no predominant color to accent. Loosen upper tension quite a bit.

Bobbin Thread - Two spools of regular thread to match fabric.

Sulky Totally Stable (iron-on tear-away temporary stabilizer) - Enough to back all areas to be sculptured.

Needles - Use size 14 Universal for regular or rayon thread.

Use size 14 Embroidery or Metallic for metallic or rayon thread.

Use size 12 Universal for clear thread.

Needle Lubricant - Necessary if using metallic thread.

Sulky Solvy or Stick-dSolv - Use if transferring a design or motif onto fleece fabric.

THINGS TO THINK ABOUT

BUTTONHOLES

Before sculpting an area that will have buttonholes, mark all of the buttonhole placements so that sculpturing stitches completely avoid the buttonholes. This applies to the garment front as well as the facings.

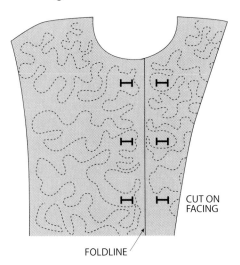

CUT ON FACING

FOLDLINE

CUT-ON FACINGS

If the garment has cut-on facings, avoid sculpturing over foldlines by marking them before "sculpturing." *Note: Stitching lines crossing the foldline may result in an uneven folded edge.*

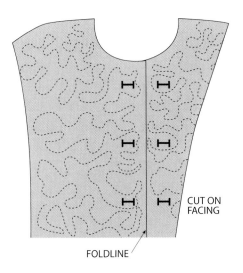

CUT ON FACING

FOLDLINE

ROLL-UP CUFFS

If the fabric has no obvious right or wrong side and the garment has roll-up cuffs that will be sculptured, fold the cuffs to finished position and mark the depth of the cuff.

In this case, the **wrong** side of the fabric will be the **visible** side of the cuff. **Stabilize on the right side** and **sculpture stitch on the wrong side** of the fabric. *(Note: This is opposite to all the other sculpturing directions.)*

PLAN OF ATTACK

1. Cut out the garment sections that are to be sculptured. Note: Sculpturing is done on cutout garment pieces before construction and on a single layer of fabric only. If there is a cut-on facing, sculpture the facing separately, avoiding stitching over the fold-line.

2. Press Sulky Totally Stable stabilizer, to wrong side of fabric, behind the area to be sculptured. Use a dry iron and light pressure.

Note: In the Basics Chapter of this book I said to never touch an iron to the surface of fleece. In this case, we are using the iron but **not touching the fleece**. Touch the iron only to the Totally Stable. Never iron directly on the fleece.

WHY PRESS-ON STABILIZER?

Most fleeces have quite a bit of stretch in at least one direction. It is imperative that we remove the stretch factor from the fabric before we begin stitching.

Pin-on stabilizer would still allow the fleece to stretch as the satin stitching is worked.

The press-on stabilizer, adhered to the fleece, becomes "one with the fabric" and does not allow the fabric to stretch during stitching. *Note: I know some people*

advocate doing this stitching without stabilization, but unless the fabric is quite stable on its own, there is too great a danger for distortion, rippling and stretching. Using Totally Stable iron-on stabilizer assures success every time.

Exception

Some shearlings have quite a stable backing and may not need the press-on stabilizer. Stitch a test sample on scrap fabric before deciding to eliminate the stabilization step.

3. Stitch the sculpturing lines on the right side of the fabric using a 3.5mm to 4mm zigzag stitch width and a shorter stitch length. This is not quite satin stitch density and a little fabric should show between the stitches.

Important

A. Do sample stitching on a stabilized scrap.

B. Adjust stitch width and density according to your machine and personal taste.

C. Experiment using different presser feet to determine which works best for the fabric and the machine you are using. You may opt to use a regular zigzag presser foot, a satin stitch appliqué presser foot or an open-toe embroidery presser foot. Note: The open-toe presser foot works better on lower loft fleeces. On higher loft fleeces, you will probably prefer using a zigzag or appliqué presser foot. The crossbar between the toes on these feet flattens the fleece in front of the needle, allowing more visibility.

D. If there is any difficulty with the fabric feeding through the machine, loosen the stitch density and/or lighten the presser foot pressure.

4. When finished sculpturing, remove stabilizer from the backside and discard.

*Note: Some stabilizer remains in the stitching, but it is on the **wrong** side of the fabric and will not be visible.*

5. Compare sculptured garment pieces to original pattern pieces and re-true edges if necessary.

OPTIONAL SCULPTURING STITCH CHOICES:

While zigzag stitching is quick and easy to sew out, other decorative stitches offer interesting effects. Choose a simple decorative stitch from the satin stitch category.

Note: Open work stitches will be lost in the loft of the fabric and intricate stitches will take "forever."

Waves, scallops, elliptical shapes and hearts are good satin stitch choices that sew quickly and offer attractive results. Just for fun, try a wavy satin stitch in a grid design (discussed later in this chapter). Browse through the sewing machine manual and experiment with a variety of stitches. Or, program a sequence of decorative satin stitches. Save some fabric scraps for playing and experimenting before doing the "real thing."

SCULPTURING DESIGN CHOICES

MEANDERING

"Meandering" is a fast and easy way to sculpture. There is no need to draw a design. Simply wander as you stitch and create jigsaw-puzzle-piece shapes. Avoid crossing over previous meandering stitching lines. Sew in one long continuous "squiggle" line. If you become "locked in a corner;" stop, tie off thread tails and begin again.

Caution: When you "meander," choose an open, flowing pattern, especially on larger

garment sections. If you sew in tight little intricate curves, you will find yourself sitting at the machine for what seems like an eternity and using tons of thread. Again, a test sample is worth the few extra minutes and will give you all necessary information.

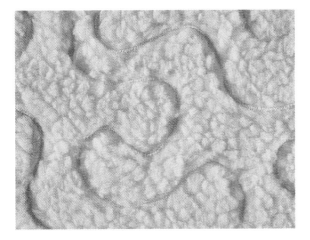

Not every nook and cranny is supposed to be identical! Don't worry that the stitch density varies around larger and smaller curves. When finished, everything will appear amazingly balanced.

This is a very, very easy technique. Turn up the music, put the pedal to the floor and lose yourself in pleasant daydreaming while "meandering" up and down and all around!

CHECKS & PLAIDS: GRIDDED LINES & PLANNED PATTERNS

I love this technique for creating a coordinate fleece "print" to go with my "solid" fleece!

This technique offers the perfect option for those who crave order and balance. A plain solid fleece can easily be turned into a check or a plaid design.

Use a "created print" for:
• contrast yokes, sleeves, collars, pockets, etc.

• making a "patterned" vest front to coordinate with the "plain" back.
• creating "patterned" sleeves to be set into a "plain" jacket body.
• Or, use this idea anywhere you believe a "contrast" area might add interest.

Plan of Attack

1. Cut out fleece garment pieces.
2. Press Sulky Totally Stable stabilizer to the wrong side of the pieces to be sculptured.
3. Hard Way: Use a Clover Chacopel pencil and a see-through ruler to draw all of the sculpturing lines. Satin stitch on the drawn lines.

Easy Way: Use a Clover Chacopel pencil to *draw only the first sculpturing line* and satin stitch. Attach a quilting bar to the presser foot, or onto the sewing machine (depending upon the machine model) and move the appropriate distance away from the needle for the next sculpturing stitching line. Use the quilt bar as a guide and continue sewing lines until the fabric piece is completely sculpture stitched.

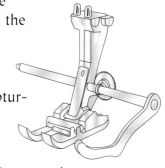

If creating boxes or checks, use a pencil and see-through ruler to draw a second line intersecting the first row at a 90° angle. Again, using the quilting bar, stitch remaining intersecting lines until the fabric is completely covered. This is quick, easy and there is no room for error!

OUTLINE SCULPTURING FOR A QUILTED LOOK

Choose a printed fleece such as a blanket print or Aztec design. The print may be used for the whole garment or for a contrast yoke or collar.

"Sculpture" the fleece by satin-stitch outlining the dominant print lines. If the print lines offer a dominant color, choose that color thread to enhance the design.

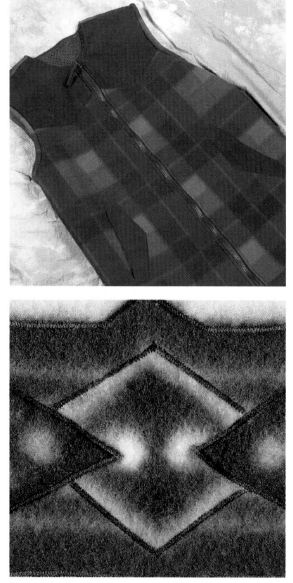

If the print is multi-colored and one thread color will interfere with the print, use clear or smoke thread for the sculpture stitching. This results in a subtle grooved look, with no color change.

Outline sculpturing results in a soft quilted appearance. When the entire garment is created from a print, consider outline stitching a couple of areas for a subtle contrast. For example: Outline sculpture the yoke, the front panels, or the collar and pockets.

SINGLE MOTIF

A single motif is a great accent for any polar jacket or top. Choose the motif according to the interests of the person who will be wearing the garment. It may be a flower motif, a sports design or a toddler's favorite storybook character. A sculptured motif is a fun addition to the whole family's wardrobe.

Note: Advertisements, wrapping paper, coloring books, sports catalogs, fabric prints and appliqué books are good sources for finding designs.

Hint: Choose a simple design that will allow space between the stitching lines to "puff" between the grooves.

Plan of Attack

1. Press Sulky Totally Stable stabilizer onto the wrong side of fleece, behind the motif area.

2. Make a design template by tracing the motif onto Sulky Solvy or Stick-dSolv water soluble stabilizer. Use a permanent marking pen, water erase fabric marker or air erase fabric marker to draw motif. Since the stabilizer will be rinsed away, it is important to make sure the ink will not stain the fabric.

3. Pin traced Solvy in place or adhere Stick-dSolv on right side of traced fabric.

4. Satin-stitch the design.

5. Tear away stabilizer from the backside of the fabric.

6. Rinse away any water-soluble stabilizer.

OVER-SIZED DESIGNS (see the "Dramatic Sculptured Jacket" in Part II)

At times a design may be too large to easily trace onto water soluble stabilizer. In such a case trace the design onto the "papery" or non-stick side of Totally Stable iron-on tear-away stabilizer, before pressing stabilizer to wrong side of fabric.

*Be Aware: Finished sculpted design will be reversed to the traced design. If the motif is a one-way design, with a right and wrong direction, **mirror image before** tracing it onto Totally Stable.*

1. Trace design onto Totally Stable, mirror-imaging, if necessary.

2. Press Totally Stable onto the wrong side of the garment, placing the design in desired position.

*3. To transfer the design to the right side of the garment for sculpture stitching, straight stitch the entire motif from the **wrong** side of garment. For better visibility, use a bobbin thread slightly darker or lighter than the fleece color. Don't worry if the stitching isn't "pretty," because you will be sculpture stitching over it. This is to be used as a guideline only.*

4. From the right side of garment, stitch the sculpturing lines, using the just-stitched bobbin thread as a guideline.

5. Because the design is large, roll up the edge of garment for easy maneuvering. With multiple handling, the Totally Stable may separate from the fleece. As necessary, press to re-adhere the Totally Stable.

POLAR PINTUCKS: BREAKING THE MOLD!

We usually don't mention "fleece" and "pintucks" in the same sentence. However, creative sewers of today have broken all the molds!

Thanks to Christina Porter for sharing this imaginative idea of combining twin needles and polar fleece. Use pintucks to create texture, stitch a design on a solid color fleece or accent a print.

Unique Ideas
- Create a cascade of pintucks falling from one shoulder.
- Center a cascade of pintucks down the center of a sleeve.
- Meander, free-form style, all over a plain pullover front.
- Design a pintucked "yoke" with parallel pintuck lines or arranged into a plaid.

- Stitch multiple rows above sleeve cuffs and garment hems to create borders.
- Frame a collar with double or triple pintucked rows.
- Liven up a plain pullover front by stitching a tic-tac-toe grid. Each gridline should three pintucked rows stitched closely together. Embellish the tic-tac-toe block centers with appliqué or embroidery designs.
- Pick up the dominant lines of a print and accent them with pintucks.
- Check & Plaids: Use the same approach as described in "Sculpturing – Checks & Plaids" in this section, and pintuck instead of sculpture stitch the design.

Requirements
4.0/90 Twin Needle - Size 4.0/100 for heavy fleece and/or for using metallic threads. Use 4.0/80 for medium weight fleece.

3-groove Pintuck Presser Foot - The grooves on the underside of this presser foot allow the welts to stay raised. Use of this foot also makes it easy to evenly space multiple rows of parallel pintucks.

Plan of Attack

1. Cut out garment pieces.

2. On a scrap piece of fabric, practice pintuck stitching lines. Use a long stitch length of 3mm to 3.5mm or 7 to 9 stitches per inch. Tighten the needle tension to produce a raised welt between the twin needle stitching lines. If the pintucks are to be sewn on both the lengthwise and crosswise grainlines, test the stitching on both grains.

3. Stitch pintucks on garment pieces.

Note: There is no stabilizer used on the backside when sewing pintucks. The beauty of pintucking is the raised welt effect. Stabilizer would prevent this effect.

Here is an area where sewing and common sense come into play. "Legally," the sewing rules say that pintucking is supposed to be done before cutting out the pattern pieces. Pintucks take up fabric in each of the little tucks, narrowing the fabric with each tuck.

On a close fitting heirloom blouse made from cotton batiste, embellished with many rows of pintucks, it is imperative to pintuck first and cut out second. Pintucking on fleece is a bit more forgiving.

First of all, the garment pattern is most likely moderate to generous in sizing. And, you are probably not doing rows upon rows of pintucking…at least not enough to significantly alter the garment size. So, unless the pintucks interfere with the garment fit, cutting out the pattern pieces first and pintucking second is the easiest order of sewing.

Be prepared to use ribbing or elastic finish at the lower edge of the garment. With some fleeces, if there is much pintucking in the hem area, the hem may tend to curl out. If you want a hem, a deeper hem will assist in counteracting this "curl-out" tendency.

BEST OF BOTH WORLDS - Sculpturing and Pintucks for the truly free-spirited!

This combination gives even more texture interest. Meander and scroll or plan an orderly, repetitive design. Whatever suits your taste!

NANCY'S CAUTION:

Combining sculpturing and pintucking offers dramatic results. However, plan the order of sewing before beginning.

Any embellishment such as sculpture stitching or embroidery that requires a stabilized back should be done first.

Pintucking, which does not require stabilization, should be done last. If the pintucks are done on a stabilized fleece, the welts can't raise. If the pintucks are done first and then the stabilizing backing is pressed on, the tucks will flatten. Plan first - sew second!

EMBROIDERING ON FLEECE

Home embroidery machines have opened up a whole new world to the home sewer. A few simple tips for embroidering on polars and your embroidery horizon will successfully expand into a whole new arena.

Just as with other embroidery projects, choose the needle size and type according to the fabric weight and the thread being used. A heavy fleece requires a larger needle and metallic threads require an embroidery or metallic needle.

Neat Tip #1
Since it is difficult to hoop fleece, if not impossible, and hooping would probably leave imprints on the fleece, you will like the convenience, and speed, of using adhesive paper in a hoop.

Filmoplast Stic, Sulky Sticky Back and Stick- It-All are a few of the choices readily available. Follow the manufacturer's directions for hooping and removal of the release paper to expose the adhesive. You will love the ability to lift and realign the fleece as necessary without the hassle of hooping and re-hooping fabric.

Important Note: Adhesive paper simply replaces the hooping process. It does not replace the need for stabilizer! Slip stabilizer under the hoop before starting to embroider.

Anita Covert, owner of **Country Stitches** in Michigan, is an embroidery expert. With her permission, I have included some terrific information from her book, *Creative Combinations*.

"Important! Important! Final Note About Stabilizers: After two and a half years of experimenting, we have concluded that the way a design is digitized influences the type and amount of stabilizer needed. Because digitizers vary in their methods of digitizing, it is often beneficial to first stitch a sample. We suggest that if you have problems with gaps between rows, puckers, or gaps between the embroidery and the outline, try re-hooping using a stiffer stabilizer or add more stabilizer."

Neat Tip #2
Pin a piece of Sulky Solvy, or adhere a piece of Stick-dSolv over the design area before you begin embroidering. This will keep the stitches laying on top of the fleece, rather then sinking down into the loft of the fabric. This also assists in keeping the stitches even and consistent and prevents any fleece hairs from poking up between the stitches. Rinse away when finished.

Neat Tip #3

A common occurrence when embroidering on fleece is the "show through" that happens when there is a strong color difference between the thread and the fleece. *For example, a white snowman embroidered on red fleece has a tendency to have hints of red showing between the white stitches.* Even if using the correct stitch density, correct needle and thread and a water soluble stabilizer as a topping, the stitches cannot be sewn close enough together to totally block out the strong color underneath.

Cover-Up is a permanent, adhesive-backed plastic vinyl film that is available in a variety of colors. Use as a topping to eliminate show-through. Match the Cover-Up color to the thread. Adhere over the area to be stitched and embroider. Tear away excess when finished.

> # NANCY'S HINT'S
>
> **Regarding Stick-dSolv, Cover-Up and all other tacky adhesives, read "A Word About Adhesives" in Chapter Two, "Basics" for some helpful information.**

APPLIQUÉ ON FLEECE

Appliqué on fleece presents a different kind of challenge. On other fabrics, appliqués are fused in place resulting in a smooth, even satin stitch.

Totally Stable does a nice job of stabilizing the fleece on the backside, but fusing the appliqué in place is risky with fleece. Fusing requires heat and pressure which, when applied to fleece, will probably leave a permanent iron imprint, or worse yet, melt the fleece.

Fuse 'n Stick is the solution to this problem. One side is fusible and the other side has a pressuer sensitive adhesive

Iron Fuse 'n Stick to the wrong side of appliqué fabric. Peel off protective paper to reveal pressure sensitive adhesive.

The adhesive holds the appliqué pieces in place on the face of the fleece while the Totally Stable stabilizes the backside.

The end result is smooth, even satin stitching with no ripples or distortion.

PART TEN

THE GALLERY

Fashioned by Kathy Osborne - Cheaters Trim Part Five.

Made by Doris Zopfi - UltraSuede Accent Part Eight.

Made by Barb Dau - Complete Directions for Backwards Zipper and Trim in Part Six.

Designed and made by Nancy Cornwell -
Taking a Commercial Pattern and Making It
Your Own Part Eleven.

Provided by Stretch & Sew Inc. - Buttonholes Part Seven.

Provided by Kwik-Sew Pattern Company - Original pattern. See page 112 for designer changes.

Designed and made by Nancy Cornwell - Buttonholes Part Seven, Sculpturing Part Nine.

Provided by Stretch & Sew Inc. - Cheaters Ribbing Wrapped Edge Part Five.

Made by Nancy Cornwell – Polar Pintucking Part Nine.

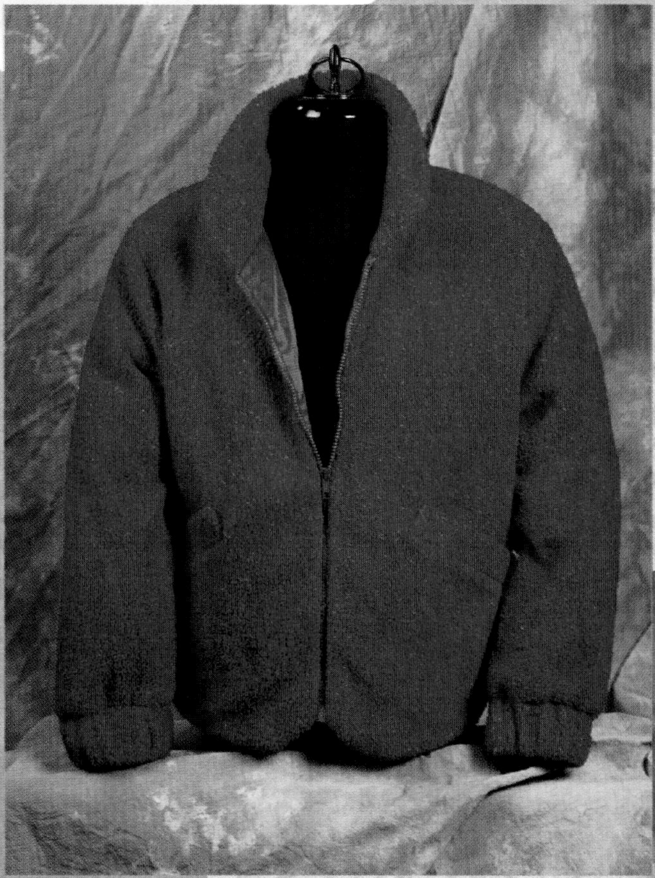

Provided by Stretch & Sew
Inc. – Zippers Part Six, Elastic
Cuffs Part Five.

Right: Designed and made by
Nancy Cornwell – Backwards
Zipper and Trim Part Six

Elegant and Easy Cape designed and made by Nancy Cornwell – Complete Directions Part Eleven.

Stadium Coat made by Paula Harvey – Sculpturing Part Nine, Blunt Edge Cut with a Wavy Rotary Cutter Part Nine.

Made by Nancy Cornwell - No-Fail Collar Part Three, Cheaters Ribbing Wrapped Edges Part Five, Ribbing Wrapped Edges with Elastic Part Five, No Hassle Zippers Part Six, No Side Seam Part Six, 5-minute Hat Happy Endings Part Eleven.

Made by Nancy Cornwell - Cheaters Ribbing Wrapped Edges Part Five, No Side Seam Part Three.

(left) Made by Sharyl Buehler. (right) Made by Sue Mitrovich.

Designed and made by Nancy Cornwell - Blunt Edge Part Four, Self Fabric Techniques Part Five.

Snuggle Bag made by Nancy Cornwell - Complete Directions Part Eleven.

Right: No Brainer Blanket made by Nancy Cornwell - Directinos Part Eleven, Quick Fringe Part Eleven.

*Made by Nancy Cornwell - No-Fail
Collar Part Three, UltraSuede Zipper
Pull Part Eight, Easy Zipper Pocket
Part Six.*

*Made by Nancy Cornwell - Lycra
Wrapped Edge ìReal Wayî Part Five,
Gridded Sculpture Stitched Yolk Part
Nine.*

Made by Linda Bartlett – Wrapped Edges Part Five, Sport Snaps Part Seven.

Diamond Lattice Pullover designed and made by Nancy Cornwell - Complete Directions Part Eleven, Templates in back.

Patchwork Pullover made by Nancy Cornwell - Directions Part Eleven.

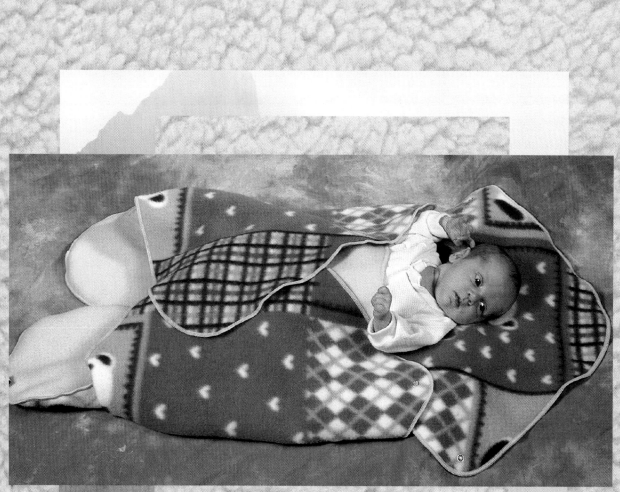

*Baby Snuggle Wrap made by Martha Mauer –
Complete Directions Part Eleven.*

*Baby Collection made by Martha Mauer – Directions Part
Eleven, Quick Fringe Part Eleven.*

Top Left: Made by Kay Wallace. Fat Piping Part Five, UltraSuede Techniques Part Eight. Bottom Left Photo (right vest): Made by Marge Hansen - Buttonloops Part Eight.

Vest made by Nancy Cornwell - Fat Piping Part Five, UltraSuede Techniques Part Eight. Pullover made by Nancy Cornwell - UltraSuede Techniques Part Eight, 5-Minute Hat Part Eleven.

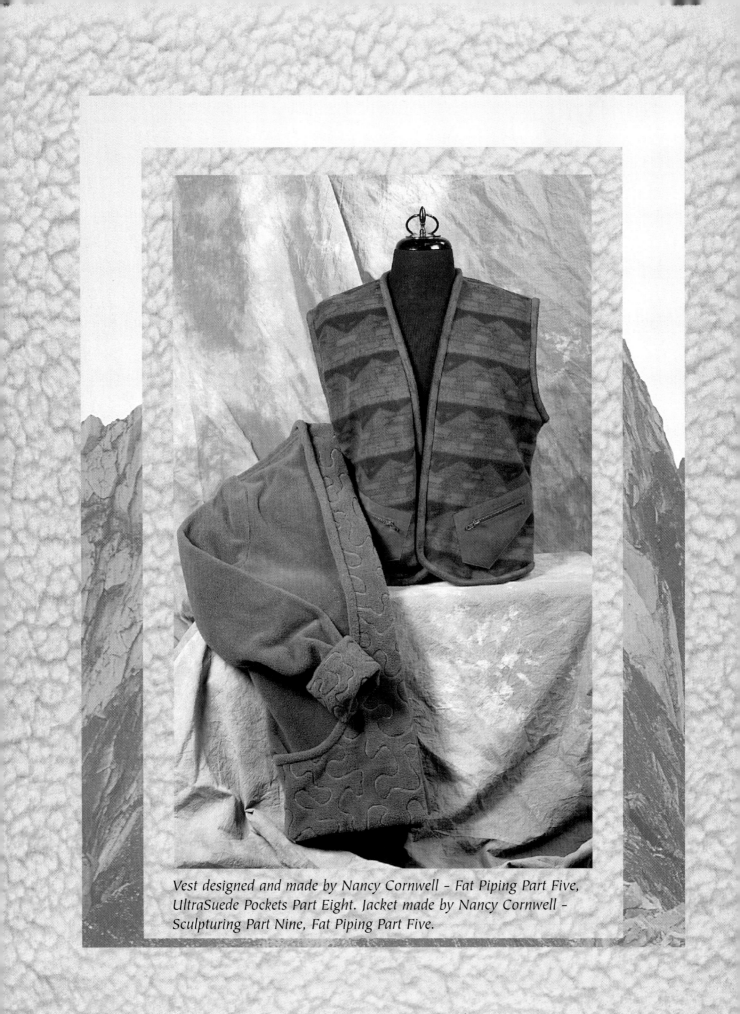

Vest designed and made by Nancy Cornwell - Fat Piping Part Five, UltraSuede Pockets Part Eight. Jacket made by Nancy Cornwell - Sculpturing Part Nine, Fat Piping Part Five.

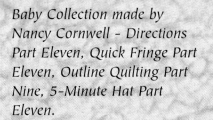

Baby Collection made by
Nancy Cornwell - Directions
Part Eleven, Quick Fringe Part
Eleven, Outline Quilting Part
Nine, 5-Minute Hat Part
Eleven.

Right: Little Lady's Polar
Wardrobe made by Nancy
Cornwell. Idea from Pat
Headen of Hartsdale Fabrics -
Directions in Part Eleven.

Clockwise from top left: 1)Provided by Kwik-Sew Pattern Company, 2)Provided by Kwik-Sew Pattern Company, 3)Child's Nap Blanket made by Sue Mitrovich, 4)Provided by Kwik-Sew Pattern Company.

PLAYING WITH POLARFLEECE®

LITTLE LADY'S POLAR WARDROBE PAGE 145

A potpourri of fun garments and items to make, incorporating ideas and techniques covered throughout the book!

Items created from Timber Lane Press Patterns.

JACKET WITH DRAMATIC SCULPTURED BACK... AND, HOW TO TAKE A COMMERCIAL PATTERN AND MAKE IT YOUR OWN

This is a dramatic sculpture design that will turn heads.
Be dramatic and choose a strong contrasting colored thread to sculpture on a bold colored fleece. Or, for pure elegance and understatement, choose similar colored thread to produce a subtle tone-on-tone effect.

Choose a favorite looser-fitting jacket pattern with one piece back. Sculpture the Scroll design on the back. *Note: A center back seam will interfere with the sculpturing design.*

Quilting stencils and Celtic designs provide excellent design choices for other projects. Quilting stencils frequently offer various sizes of the same motif. Choose a smaller version to embellish a shirt front and use the larger version for a dramatic back embellishment. Or, repeat a motif, sprinkled down one side of a vest.

Included throughout this book, are ideas for making changes to commercial patterns. Following are examples of how to combine and use some of the ideas presented or "**How to take a commercial pattern and make it your own.**"

The red coat pictured on page 113 is made exactly "according to pattern" using Kwik Sew pattern #2560. It is a reversible coat, red Berber print reversing to solid black fleece. The royal jacket (shorter view, same pattern) incorporates many of the techniques and ideas featured throughout this book.

CHANGES

1. Single layer (rather than reversible).
2. Add UltraSuede piping in front, center and back sleeve seams.
3. Blunt edge finish for the collar. (If fleece is thick enough for a good blunt edge this reduces seam allowance bulk.)
4. Contrast roll-up cuffs.
5. Add dramatic sculpture design on the back.
6. Add Ultra Suede buttonhole patches and loops. (To replace traditional buttonholes.)
7. Sculpture stitch, UltraSuede, contrast cuff and buttons are all from a contrast color.

REQUIREMENTS
Fabric - main color according to pattern envelope back
1/4 yard contrast fabric for collar/cuffs
Notions per pattern envelope back
Decorative thread for sculpturing
Thread to match fleece color
Thread one shade darker or lighter than fleece color for stitch transferring sculpture design
2 yards Totally Stable iron-on tear-away stabilizer
5" x 45" UltraSuede
Basting Tape or Fuse 'N Stick to adhere buttonhole patches.

Use 1/4" seam allowance.

1. Cut out garment according to pattern directions, making the following changes:

   A. For 2" hem, lengthen 2" at lower edge. (Changing from reversable to hemmed garment).

   B. Use the front interfacing pattern piece and widen it to 5." Cut two for front facings.

   C. Since the collars will be sewn with a blunt edge finish, the edges should be perfect and neat.

   1. Trace a "whole" collar pattern piece (rather than using the given "cut on fold" pattern piece).

   2. Use a rotary cutter to cut collars double layer, **wrong** sides together. This method assures that the edges are exactly even and ready to sew.

   3. When cutting the collars from contrast fabric, place pattern pieces closer to one selvage edge, leaving the extra fabric for the cuffs.

   Note: The cuffs will be cut out during construction.

2. Use a Chacopel pencil and draw a center back line on **wrong** side of back. Draw a horizontal line intersecting center back line at the desired position for the center of your sculpturing design.

3. Use a lead pencil to trace the larger scroll design four times onto the papery side of Totally Stable stabilizer: Two times "as is" and two times "mirror imaged." *Note: To mirror image, turn design over and trace from the backside.*

   Trace the smaller scroll twice, once "as is" and once "mirror imaged." Use a light box or tape the design against a window. *(Template in back of book.)*

4. Use the drawn placement lines as a guide for centering the sculpturing designs. Press the traced Totally Stable designs onto the **wrong** side of the garment back. Refer to photograph for placement.

5. Stitch transfer sculpture design. See directions in Part 9 - Designer Details, Oversized Designs.

6. From the **right** side of the garment, stitch the scroll sculpturing lines using a 3mm to 4mm zigzag stitch width and a shorter stitch length. Note: This is not quite a satin stitch density. A little fabric should show between the stitches. Experiment on a scrap until you have the desired stitch width and density.

   A. Note: Roll up edges of jacket to keep garment out of the way when sculpturing.

   B. With all the handling, it will be necessary to periodically re-press the Totally Stable to re-adhere.

   C. Experiment with different presser feet to determine which gives the best visibility for stitching around the curves.

   D. Don't be too hard on yourself when the stitching isn't perfect (the curves won't be perfect). Before you consider ripping out any stitching and re-doing, finish entire motif first. The "whole" looks great, whereas many of the "individual parts" may not look so great.

NANCY'S HINT:

For in-depth sculpturing information, sample stitching, which presser foot to use, etc. Refer to Part 9 – Designer Details.

7. Tear away stabilizer from the backside and discard.

8. Cut six 1/2" x 45" strips of UltraSuede for piping. See Part 8.

9. Sew **front** to **front sleeve** with piping sandwiched between. *Note: The **wrong** side of UltraSuede piping should be against the **right** side of **front**.* Finger press seam allowances toward the **front sleeve** and topstitch at a scant 1/4".

10. Sew **back** to **back sleeve** with piping sandwiched between. *Note: The **wrong** side of UltraSuede piping should be against the **right** side of **back**.* Finger press seam allowances towards **back sleeve** and topstitch at a scant 1/4".

11. Sew **front sleeve** to **back sleeve** with piping sandwiched between. *Note: The **wrong** side of UltraSuede piping should be against the **right** side of **back sleeve**.* Finger press seam allowances towards **front sleeve** and topstitch at a scant 1/4".

12. Sew **pockets** and **side seams** according to pattern directions.

13. For a blunt edge finish, sew the **collar wrong** sides together by edge-stitching outer edges at 1/8".

14. Baste **collar** to **neck edge**. Match notches according to pattern directions.

15. If desired, serger finish inside edge of **front facing**.

16. Use a conventional sewing machine - **Right** sides together, sew **front facing** to **front**, sandwiching basted **collar** at neck edge. Continue stitching to center back. At lower edge, sew across **facing** 2" above bottom edge for hem. Trim **facing** only.

17. Turn **front facing** to finished position.

18. Blind-hem stitch a 2" hem at lower edge. Use a 4mm long and 4mm wide stitch.

19. Topstitch, using a 1/4" seam allowance, up center front and around to center back neck. On both sides, begin at **lower edge** and end at **center back**.

20. Draw a pattern piece for **contrast cuff** 5" wide x the circumference of the sleeve at the hem edge, plus 1/2".

21. Cut two **cuffs** from contrast fleece.

22. Sew cuffs into a circle.

23. **Right** sides together, sew **cuff** to **sleeve** edge.

24. Turn **cuff** to inside the **sleeve**. Slightly roll the seam towards the **sleeve**.

25. Stitch upper edge of **cuff** (unsewn edge) to **sleeve**.

26. Turn **sleeve** to finished position. Roll up 3" contrast **cuff**.

27. Cut three triangles for **buttonhole patches** from UltraSuede. Make UltraSuede **buttonhole loops**. (See Part 8.)

28. Use wash-away basting tape or Fuse 'N Stick according to pattern directions for buttonhole placement to arrange and adhere patches and loops. Edgestitch to secure. (See Part 8.)

29. Sew buttons in place. For added security, slip squares of interfacing between the **facing** and the **front** in the button sew-on area. Or, back the button with an additional small flat button on the **wrong** side.

NANCY'S HINT:

For more consistent corners, take two diagonal stitches instead of pivoting sharply. This will soften the corners, making them easier to trim and turn.

NANCY'S HINT:

After trimming the corners, if a serger is available, serge the front seam and neck seam for a more compact seam allowance area.

DIAMOND LATTICE APPLIQUÉ

"Bring polar in from the cold."

Polar fabrics are not just for the outdoors anymore. This warm, cuddly fabric is an ideal choice for pullovers, sweatshirts and sweaters. "Dress it up" by adding a touch of UltraSuede appliqué.

You'll love the clever way the UltraSuede is cut out and the simple way the appliqué pieces are arranged.

This design is appropriate for sweaters, sweatshirts, plain front pullovers, dresses and even denim jacket backs. Using the same clever UltraSuede cutting approach, take this a step further to copy quilting stitch designs and interlocking Celtic designs.

This appliqué is especially striking when made from rich black UltraSuede appliquéd onto bold colored fleece.

REQUIREMENTS

1 plain front pullover garment, cut out
1/4 yard UltraSuede (enough to appliqué two garments)
Thread to match fabric and UltraSuede
Fabric glue stick or Fuse 'n Stick (to adhere appliqué in place)

FYI:

Who's to question where sewers get their ideas from?

The Diamond Lattice appliqué was inspired by the parquet design inlay on Barb Cornwell's (my sister-in-law) dining room floor. (How's that for a round-about way to find an appliqué design?) I spied this seemingly intricate motif in the corner and sketched it on a napkin. I knew that some day I would figure out what to do with it.

That day has come!

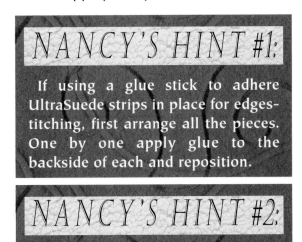

NANCY'S HINT #1:

If using a glue stick to adhere UltraSuede strips in place for edgestitching, first arrange all the pieces. One by one apply glue to the backside of each and reposition.

NANCY'S HINT #2:

If using Fuse 'n Stick, iron to the wrong side of UltraSuede before cutting pieces. Arrange pieces, then, one by one, peel off protective paper and reposition.

1. Per templates given, trace Diamond Lattice appliqué pieces (#1, #2, #3, & #4) on separate paper. Compare pattern pieces to the garment and lengthen, where indicated, to reach the shoulder edge

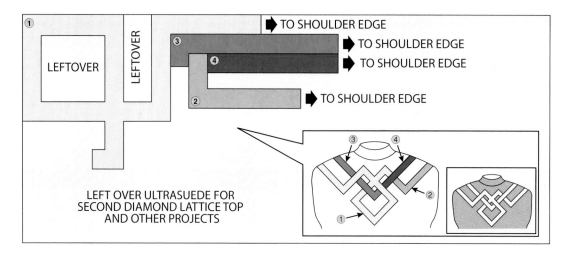

2. From UltraSuede, cut applique pieces #1, #2, #3, & #4 according to cutting diagram. All cuts are 1" wide.

3. Place UltraSuede appliqué piece #1 on garment front. Align center fronts and allow for a flattering placement below neckline. *Note:*

When planning the placement, be sure to allow for neckline trimming and suggested seam allowance on pattern.

4. Arrange appliqué pieces #2, #3 and #4 per diagram. Overlap and underlap as shown.

5. Use a glue stick or Fuse 'n Stick to adhere pieces to fleece.

6. Edgestitch UltraSuede in place, stitching along both edges of appliqué pieces.

7. Finish garment according to pattern directions.

MAKE IT YOUR WAY NO SIDE SEAM VEST

   This is a sample idea of how to combine a variety of ideas and directions found throughout this book.

1. Cut out your favorite vest pattern. If you prefer a garment with no side seams, to preserve a print design or eliminate excess bulk, see the directions in Part 3 – Simple Design Changes.

2. Apply Fat Piping finish according to directions in Part 5 – Ready-To-Wear Edge Finishes. Choose the "Order of Sewing" according to whether the vest is traditional or without side seams.

3. Add the Ultra-Easy Zippered Pocket according to directions in Part 8 – Touch Of Class UltraSuede Accents.

   A variation of these ideas can be applied to a cardigan: Apply self-fabric around outer edges of cardigan and at sleeve cuffs. Apply a single zippered chest pocket and two side patch pockets. Or, have fun and tumble three different shaped zippered pockets down the left front of a cardigan. Your only limitation is your imagination!

ELEGANT & EASY POLAR CAPE

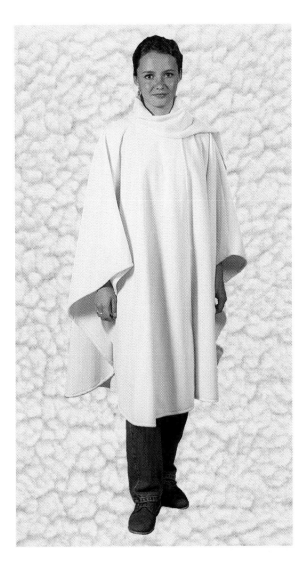

   2 1/2 yards of Polarfleece + One Hour Sewing Time = One Go-Over-Everything Cape
   Choose solid white or cream for pure "elegance." Choose a darker solid for "practicality." Or be daring and choose a sensational print...just for fun!

   Pattern: Draw Front and Back per grid (1 Square = 1"), and scarf per diagram.

REQUIREMENTS

2 1/2 yards 60" Polarfleece with no obvious right or wrong side

Note: Some fleeces are narrow. If using a narrow fabric, the "sleeve" length will be shorter.

Thread to match

Decorative thread for scarf rolled edge finish, optional

Large coat snap (for neck closure)

CUT *Note: Carefully mark **right** side of fabric.*

2 Fronts

1 Back (on fold)

1 Scarf - Cut with the fabric right side up and scarf pattern piece right side up.

CONSTRUCTION

1. Use 1/4" seam allowance and sew front to back at shoulder seam.

2. Serger finish outer edges of cape. Turn under 1/2" and topstitch at 3/8". When top-stitching, at the bottom corner edge at center front, fold center front edge over bottom edge.

3. Roll edge finish the scarf from the notch on one side to the blunt angled edge, then back to the notch on the other side.

4. **Right** sides together, sew **one** raw edge of the pointed end of scarf to the **left** side of the cape neck edge, as when wearing,. Sew the single scarf layer to the neck edge from the **left** center front, around back neck and to the **right** center front.

5. Finish the scarf inside neck edge by hand: Fold scarf in half, wrong sides together and fold under 1/2" hem allowance on the unfinished scarf edge. Hand catch stitch to the neck seamline.

6. When reaching the **right** center front, fold both rolled edges to the inside, and continue hand catch stitching for 4". Tie off and leave the rest of the rolled-edge finished scarf hanging freely.

7. Sew the **male** half of the snap onto the scarf at the **left** center **front**. Sew the **female** half of the snap on the **wrong** side (inside edge) of the scarf, 4" from the **right** center **front**.

To wear: Snap the snap, toss the scarf over your shoulder and enjoy the compliments!

SCARF DETAIL

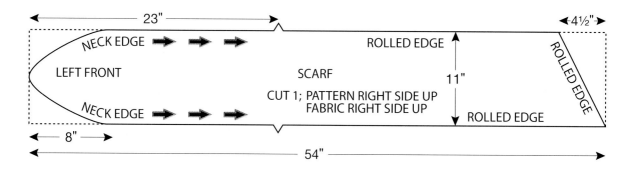

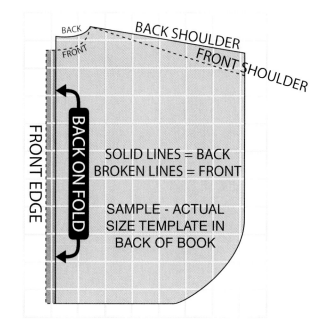

BACK

FRONT

BACK SHOULDER

FRONT SHOULDER

FRONT EDGE

BACK ON FOLD

SOLID LINES = BACK
BROKEN LINES = FRONT

SAMPLE - ACTUAL
SIZE TEMPLATE IN
BACK OF BOOK

PATCHWORK PULLOVER: (USING THE POLAR PIECING TECHNIQUE)

A great way to use up leftover polar pieces and get a warm, cuddly pullover, too!

Use polar scraps to make patchwork yardage for the garment front and accent the intersections with decorative Sport Snaps. Solid color sleeves, back, and ribbing complete the garment.

Polar piecing is a quilting technique that adjoins polar-type scraps together into usable fabric pieces. This technique dramatically changes the look of any sewing project. To secure intersections, simply add snaps where corners meet.

In this garment idea, squares are pieced together, but any shapes that fit together (squares, triangles, rectangles) will work. Consult your favorite quilting reference book for design possibilities.

Polar Piecing looks great when used for jackets, pullovers, vests, pillows, etc. When finished sewing a pullover, don't toss out those leftovers! Leftovers are perfect for Flip Flop Slippers because the fabric has already been created! (Slipper pattern from The Snap Source.)

REQUIREMENTS

A plain front pullover sweatshirt style pattern

1 1/4 to 1 1/2 yards of the main color - enough for sleeves and back

Assortment of leftover polar pieces cut into 3 1/2" squares for patchwork piecing

Patchwork color options:

Two-color theme: One color matches sleeves and back, the second color is contrast. Accent Sport Snaps in main color. For example: Red and black patchwork, black sleeves, back, ribbing and snaps.

Three-color theme: Two contrast colors complimenting the main color. Accent Sport Snaps in the main color. For example: Red and royal patchwork, black sleeves, back, ribbing and snaps.

Multi-color theme: Toss in all the colors from your scrap heap and piece in random order. Choose a main color that compliments them all. Accent Sport Snaps in the main color. Ribbing according to pattern requirments 3 to 4 dozen, size 16 Sport Snaps

1. Trace one whole garment front onto pattern tracing material. Draw in center front line. *Note: skip this step if the pattern offers a full front pattern piece.*
2. Cut polar pieces for the patchwork front into exact 3 1/2" squares.

Note: These squares can be larger or smaller depending upon personal preference or the size of scraps available.

NANCY'S HINT:

As mentioned in the "Basics" chapter, be consistent in keeping the "right sides out." Rather than meticulously mark each and every square, just cut each piece "right side up" and stack the pieces "right side up." This will assure consistency when grabbing each one to sew.

3. Alternating colors, butt edges of squares and sew strips of 3 1/2" squares together. Sew strips 10 squares long. If necessary, trim edges to neaten.

NANCY'S HINT:

To make this step quick and easy, use your Edgestitch Presser Foot. Place the "blade" between the squares. Push the squares together, and sew using an "open" type stitch. For security, use a multiple zigzag, serpentine, universal stitch, or other "open" stitch rather than a simple zigzag stitch. Stitch width must be a minimum of 4mm wide. (Wider is even better.)

4. Working on a flat surface, lay the strips alongside each other. Arrange so that the color squares alternate across and up-and-down.

Note: Do not sew strips together yet!

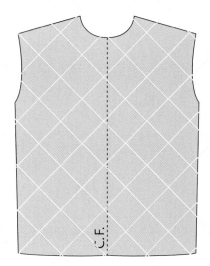

5. According to diagram, lay the **front** pattern piece on top of the strips. Use the center front line to bisect the squares. If the strips are not long enough to extend beyond the pattern piece, add more squares where needed.

6. Continue sewing strips of squares. Check to be sure that each strip is long enough to reach beyond the edges of the **front** pattern piece. Continue building until enough strips have been made for the whole **front**.

7. Butt the strips together, offsetting squares so that they alternate colors in both directions. Sew strips together with an "open" type stitch.

8. Lay **front** pattern piece on diamond-pieced fabric. Cut out the **front**.

9. Follow manufacturer's directions and apply size 16 Sport Snaps at each intersection. This is for added security and for visual interest. Use only the decorative enamel portion of the snap, backed with the female portion of the snap.

10. Finish garment according to pattern instructions.

SNUGGLE BAG

A warm, cuddly, sack that is perfect for curling up and reading a book or watching a favorite television program.
Save energy! Turn down the thermostat and stay warm in a Polarfleece cocoon. It's the prefect gift to give to a sewing friend, or keep for yourself. Keep in mind, that at a later date, you will still have 2 1/2 yards of uncut fleece and a coordinating zipper that can be sewn into a garment!

REQUIREMENTS
2 1/2 yards fleece (suggested fabrics: Polarfleece, Berber, Sherpa)
Two cones decorative serger thread
30" zipper
Wash-away basting tape

1. With a rotary cutter, trim selvage edges from long sides of fleece. *Note: The raw edge will be visible next to the zipper.*

2. A. Slightly curve the upper edges of Snuggle Bag.

B. With a fabric marker, mark both sides 42" above the bottom edge.

C. With decorative thread in both loopers, serger finish the upper portion of the Snuggle Bag, above the 42" side marks.

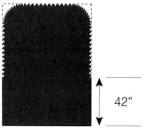

42"

3. **Right** sides together, sew center front seam from the lower edge up to the 42" marks. Use a 1/4" seam allowance.

4. **Right** sides together, center the center front seam and sew across bottom edge of the Snuggle Bag with 1/4" seam allowance.

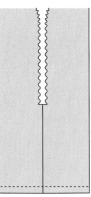

5. On the **right** side of the zipper, apply basting tape along outer edges of zipper tape.

6. Turn the Snuggle Bag **right** side out. Spread open the center front opening and insert the zipper and adhere in place. Align the decorative-stitched edge of fleece alongside the zipper teeth.

7. Stitch zipper in place. Stitch along the outer edge of decorative serger stitching.

"NO-BRAINER" BLANKET

Featuring a super easy fringing technique! Talk about quick...no sewing, just cutting!

A practical and appreciated gift for the boat, college dorm or just for curling up and watching television. This is a perfect idea for using a dynamic print that you really love but don't have enough courage to actually wear! There is no need to finish the raw edges since fleece does not ravel or fray.

REQUIREMENTS

1 1/2 to 2 yards of a bold, dramatic print
1. Use a rotary cutter and trim both selvage edges.
2. Fringe both ends with 1/2" wide fringe.

QUICK & EASY FRINGING TECHNIQUE

REQUIREMENTS

1 large cutting mat
1 small cutting mat
1. Lay fleece on the larger cutting mat.
2. Lay small cutting mat on fleece, 2 1/2" away from short end of fleece (end to be fringed).

3. Fold fleece to be fringed over the small mat.

4. Use a rotary cutter to cut 1/2" fringe. Cut from small mat and "run" onto to the large mat.

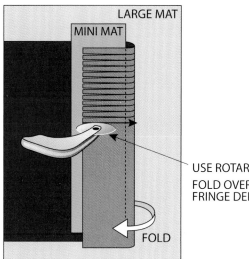

SERGER BLANKET FINISHING STITCH

Since fleece doesn't ravel, finishing the long raw side edges of the blanket is not necessary. However, if you like blanket stitching, use yarn and sew this decorative stitch by hand or try this serger technique.

Note: All sergers are different. Experiment first on scraps of fleece. Change tensions until an acceptable appearance is achieved.

1. Remove inside needle for a wide three thread stitch.

2. Set stitch length and cutting width for the widest and longest stitch available.

3. Use Décor 6 thread in a size 100/16 needle.

4. When threading the needle, do not put the needle thread in the tension disc.

5. Use Woolly Nylon in both loopers.

6. Completely tighten both loopers.

Note: Depending upon the serger, you may have to increase the looper tensions, using your fingers.

NAPTIME BUDDY – MADE TO "FIT"

What little person wouldn't love to curl up with a favorite friend?

Naptime Buddy is the perfect "bedfellow" for afternoon rest-time at daycare, a weekend trip to Grandma's house or family television time. Add a nice personal touch by machine stitching the child's name on an ear or paw. This clever idea came from Sue Mitrovich, who made this friendly lion for her special granddaughter, Jacquelyn Jenkins.

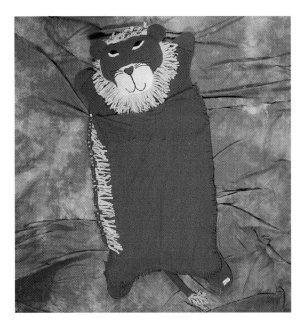

If you are artistic by nature, design your own pillow character, using as a theme the child's favorite animal, cartoon or movie personality. Otherwise, choose a fun commercial pattern for a child's pillow (like Kwik Sew #2339) as a starting point. If necessary, enlarge or reduce.

The mat is a double layer of fleece, softened with a layer or two of polyester batting. The single layer blanket is sewn to the mat along one side. The pillow is completely sewn, then attached to the mat. The child will love being "traced around" so that they can be "fitted" for their own special sleeping mat…

REQUIREMENTS
Polar-type fleece 60" fabric: 1 1/2 to 2 times the child's height for the sleeping mat
Fleece colors and yardage as required for the pillow
Contrast color fleece blanket - child's height
Stuffing for the pillow
Batting for the sleeping mat
Thread for detail stitching on pillow

1. Using a large piece of paper, pattern tracing material, butcher paper or newsprint, have the child lay on the paper and "outline" the body.

2. Using this "outline" as a starting point. Draw a sleeping mat pattern and make appropriate additions for the character or animal you are sewing (paws, tail, wings, etc.). Use the animal paws or wings to extend to 30" wide, fully using half the fleece width.

3. Draw a pattern for the "blanket" by measuring from the neck area to the end of sleeping mat by the width of the main body of the mat.

4. Stitch or appliqué facial features. Sew the pillow. Stuff pillow and finish completely.

5. Cut two layers of fleece and desired layers of batting the same shape as the drawn mat pattern.

6. Appliqué and sew any necessary details to the top layer of fleece (claws, nails, wings, tails, etc.).

7. Place the two layers of fleece **right** sides together. Place the batting layers on top of the **wrong** side of fleece. Sew around the edges and leave an opening for turning. Sew through all fleece and batting layers.

8. Turn sleeping mat to finished position and sew the opening to close.

9. Fringe the top, left and bottom edge of the blanket. Cut the fringe 1 1/2" deep. (See Quick Fringe technique on pages 142 & 143.)

10. Sew the blanket along the right side of the sleeping mat.

11. Sew the pillow onto the sleeping mat.

LITTLE LADY'S POLAR WARDROBE

*Thanks to Pat Headen, owner of **Hartsdale Fabrics** in New York, for this quick and easy idea for that special little girl in your life.*

1 1/4 yards of Polarfleece + 1 1/2 hour sewing time = Kilt, Vest, Scarf, and Hat

REQUIREMENTS
1 1/4 yards of fleece
1 1/4" sport elastic (waist measurement)
1 kilt pin, or a large gold or silver "safety pin"

KILT
1. Cut a rectangle according to diagram.

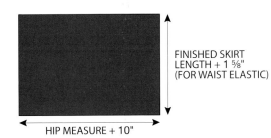

FINISHED SKIRT LENGTH + 1 ⅝" (FOR WAIST ELASTIC)

HIP MEASURE + 10"

2. Use a rotary cutter or sharp scissors to make 2 1/2" cuts, 1/2" apart at the lower edge to create "fringe." *Hint: See the "No-Brainer" Blanket in this chapter for a quick and easy fringe-cutting technique.*

3. Use pinking shears or a pinking rotary blade to "pink" the **right** side and upper edge of kilt.

RIGHT SIDE OF FABRIC

2 ½"

4. Lap **right** edge (pinked edge) 6" over **left** edge. Baste together at the upper edge.
5. Cut the elastic 3" less than waist measurement. Sew into a circle. Quarter elastic and quarter upper edge of kilt. Mark quarter marks with pins.
6. Per figure, match quarter marks and pin elastic to the **wrong** side of kilt. Place top edge of elastic 3/8" below pinked waist edge of kilt.

WRONG SIDE OF FABRIC

7. Use a 4mm long straight stitch to sew elastic to kilt with four evenly spaced rows of stitching. Stretch elastic to fit skirt. Steam to return elastic to return to original length.
8. Secure overlap with Kilt Pin.

5-MINUTE HAT
1. Use the 5-Minute Hat pattern included this chapter and cut from all one color. Or, combine with colors from your scrap stash.
2. Add an accent or two:
   A. Accent top of the hat with a small button.

B. Accent top of hat with two 1" x 7" strips of polar tied once. Angle cut the ends and leave the tails dangling.

C. Space a fun assortment of buttons around the hatband.

D. Accent hat with a Flower Pin made from fleece. See Flower Pin directions given at the end of this chapter in Happy Endings.

VEST

1. Use the "No-Side Seam Vest" directions to cut out your favorite vest pattern.

2. Sew the shoulder seams.

3. "Pink" outer edges and armholes or turn under 1/2" and topstitch.

SCARF

From the remaining fabric, cut a 6" to 8" wide and 30" to 40" long piece for the scarf. The scarf size will be dependent upon the amount of remaining fabric and the size of the child. Use a rotary cutter or sharp scissors to make 2 1/2" cuts, 1/2" apart to fringe both short ends.

BABY COLLECTION – BLANKET, PILLOW, APPLIQUÉ & TOY

The perfect gift for the new parents, or parents-to-be...And only minutes to make!

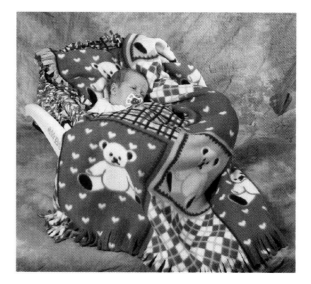

REQUIREMENT

1 1/2 yards baby print fleece

BABY BLANKET

1. Use a rotary cutter to trim selvages from both long sides of fleece.

2. Depending upon the print, cut approximately a 12" to 15" strip away from one long side of trimmed fleece. *Note: If working with a patchwork or animal print, the print will determine a usable width to cut.* Set aside for the pillow, appliqué and toy.

3. Use the "Quick & Easy Fringing Technique" on page 143 to fringe the short ends of the blanket.

BABY PILLOW

1. From the cut strip, cut two squares for a pillow. If applicable, center an animal or patchwork print.

2. For a quilted affect, sculpture stitch the outlines of the print. See "Designer Details".

3. Fringe all four sides of the pillow using

the "Quick & Easy Fringing Technique" on page 143.

4. Wrong sides together, sew pillow pieces on three sides. Sew just inside the fringe.

5. Stuff pillow with polar scraps, stuffing or a pillow form.

6. Sew remaining side of pillow.

BABY APPLIQUÉ

1. Cut out a motif from the fleece print for the appliqué. If there is not an appropriate motif, draw and cut out a simplistic heart, rattle, star or flower to create your own appliqué design.

2. Make the new baby a little sweatshirt and appliqué the motif to coordinate with the blanket. (See Part 9 - Applique for fleece.)

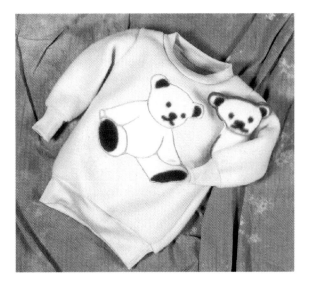

BABY TOY

1. From the fleece print, cut out two of the same motif designs.

2. Place motifs **wrong** sides together. Insert a little bit of stuffing or polar scraps to "plump" the toy. If desired, insert a plastic squeaker.

3. Edge-stitch around outer raw edges.

BABY SNUGGLE WRAP

Thanks to Grandma Martha Maurer for this idea. She saw this in a better department store and knew it would be "quick-as-a-wink" to make and at quite a dramatic savings.

This is a simply clever, footed blanket which is designed to keep a baby "toasty" while securely strapped in the car seat, stroller, infant swing or backpack. This blanket wraps the baby snug and warm and still allows the car seat shoulder straps to buckle between the legs.

Snaps can be snapped two ways: To form a hood and shoulder wrap or to fasten hood snaps to shoulder snaps, forming modified sleeves to free the hands of toddlers.

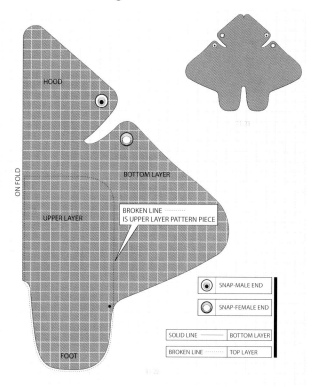

REQUIREMENTS
1 3/4 yards fleece with no obvious right or wrong side. For two-tone Snuggle Wrap (as pictured) you need: 1 1/8 yard main color and 2/3 yard contrast color

2 cones of thicker decorative thread for serger edge finish

Regular thread

1. Draw a Snuggle Blanket bottom layer and Snuggle Blanket upper layer according to diagram. One square = 1".

2. Cut out one bottom layer on the fold and one upper layer on the fold.

3. With decorative thread in both loopers and regular thread in the left needle, three thread serger finish the upper edge of the upper layer, from dot to dot.

4. **Wrong** sides together, lay upper layer on bottom layer and match edges of feet.

5. Serger finish entire perimeter. Catch both layers in the footed area.

6. Attach Sport Snaps according to diagram.

To use, lay the baby on the Snuggle Blanket. Slip the baby's feet between the double-layered feet. Tuck the upper layer around tummy and wrap around to baby's back. Wrap the sides of the Snuggle Blanket over the baby. Snap for desired configuration.

HOOD

BOTTOM LAYER

ON FOLD

UPPER LAYER

BROKEN LINE
IS UPPER LAYER PATTERN PIECE

FOOT

⊙	SNAP-MALE END
◎	SNAP-FEMALE END

SOLID LINE ————	BOTTOM LAYER
BROKEN LINE ·········	TOP LAYER

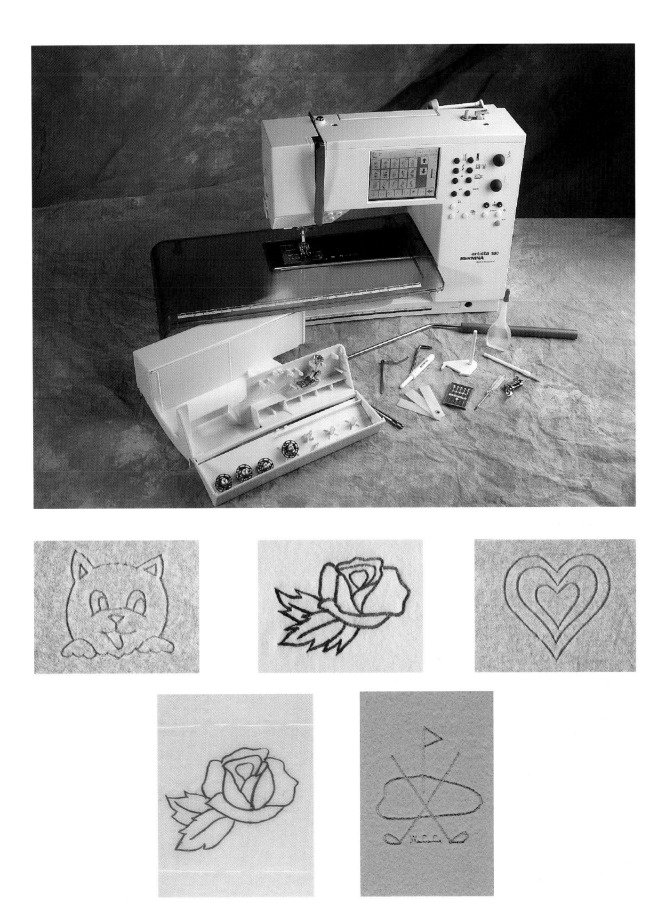

HAPPY ENDINGS – WHAT TO DO WITH LEFTOVERS

Fleece is an "environmentally friendly" and "politically correct" fabric because every scrap is truly recyclable!

Leftovers can be made into scarves, mittens, slippers and socks, headbands and hats, using any great commercial pattern (Stretch & Sew and Kwik Sew are especially good). Fun specialty patterns by Timberlane Press, or books such as *Polarfleece Pizzazz* and *More Polarfleece Pizzazz* are also good sources for patterns.

PATCHWORK YARDAGE

Follow the directions for the Patchwork Pullover on page 141 given earlier in this chapter. Create patchwork yardage for vest fronts, pillow tops, slipper tops, jackets, etc. Since the edges are just butted together and sewn, it is not a particularly strong seam and will not stand up to heavy-duty use.

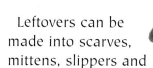

5-MINUTE HAT

1. Use the pattern templates given in the back and cut four wedges of fleece fabric in the same or alternating colors.

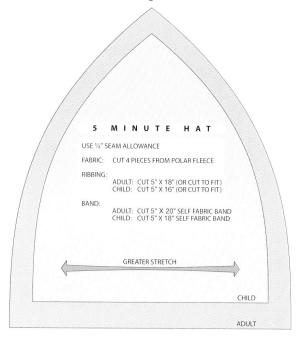

5 MINUTE HAT

USE ¼" SEAM ALLOWANCE

FABRIC: CUT 4 PIECES FROM POLAR FLEECE

RIBBING:
        ADULT: CUT 5" X 18" (OR CUT TO FIT)
        CHILD: CUT 5" X 16" (OR CUT TO FIT)

BAND:
        ADULT: CUT 5" X 20" SELF FABRIC BAND
        CHILD: CUT 5" X 18" SELF FABRIC BAND

GREATER STRETCH

CHILD

ADULT

2. Sew two wedges together, from bottom edge to point, to make one half of the hat.
3. For the other half, sew the other two wedges together.
4. Sew the two half hats together.

5. Sew ribbing or self-fabric band into a circle. The greater stretch must be in the length. Fold in half and sew to hat.

6. Add an accent to the top of the hat: a button, tassel, pom-pom, or two 1" x 7" strips tied in a knot with tails left dangling.

6-MINUTE HAT – VARIATION OF THE 5-MINUTE HAT

Cut six wedges instead of four. The result is more of a beret or a tam appearance.

SIMPLE SCARF OR MUFFLER

Use 1/4 yard of fleece or whatever you have left by the width of the fabric. Trim the selvages and fringe the short ends. It couldn't be easier!

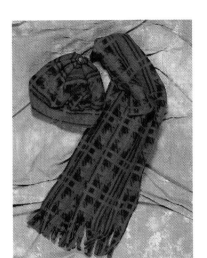

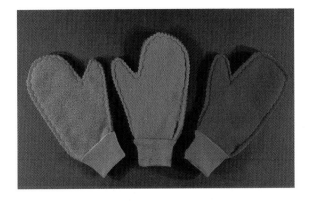

Let your little ones dig through your scrap stash and pick out their favorite colors. The mitten top can be a different color from the mitten bottom and the right hand can be different from the left hand. The ribbing can be yet an entirely different color. These aren't high-tech, just fun!

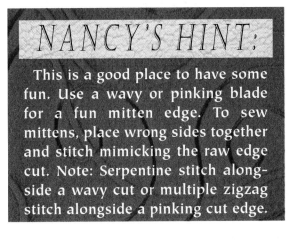

1. Place the child's hand on a piece of paper and trace outline.

2. Add a little "wiggle" room and then add 1/4" for seam allowance.

3. Cut out four mittens (two tops and two bottoms).

4. Use ribbing or nylon Lycra for cuffs. Let your little ones show off their newest mittens that they "helped make."

FLOWER PINS

Use as a fun pin on a coat or vest, or as an accent on the 5-Minute Hat band.

1. Spiral cut from a fleece with no obvious **right** or **wrong** side.
2. Cut two leaves from contrast fleece.
3. Run gathering stitches along dotted lines.

4. Pull the stitches to gather the fleece.
5. Begin with the pointed end as the center of the flower. Twist and gather the fleece into a flower shape and tie the thread tails. Hand stitch the flower together on the bottom.
6. Use a glue gun to apply glue to the backside of flower. Attach leaves and glue to a jewelry pin back.

LAST... BUT NOT LEAST

After you've created mittens, hats, pins and scarves, use the remaining bits and pieces as stuffing for all of your craft projects, pillows and stuffed animals. Fleece is truly a completely recyclable product!

Since we've now accounted for every scrap...Every inch...Every speck of fleece... We must be at the end of the book!

Happy Sewing!

Love,
Marcy

THIS POINT IS
CENTER OF FLOWER

SPIRAL CUT FOR FLOWER

LEAF CUT 2

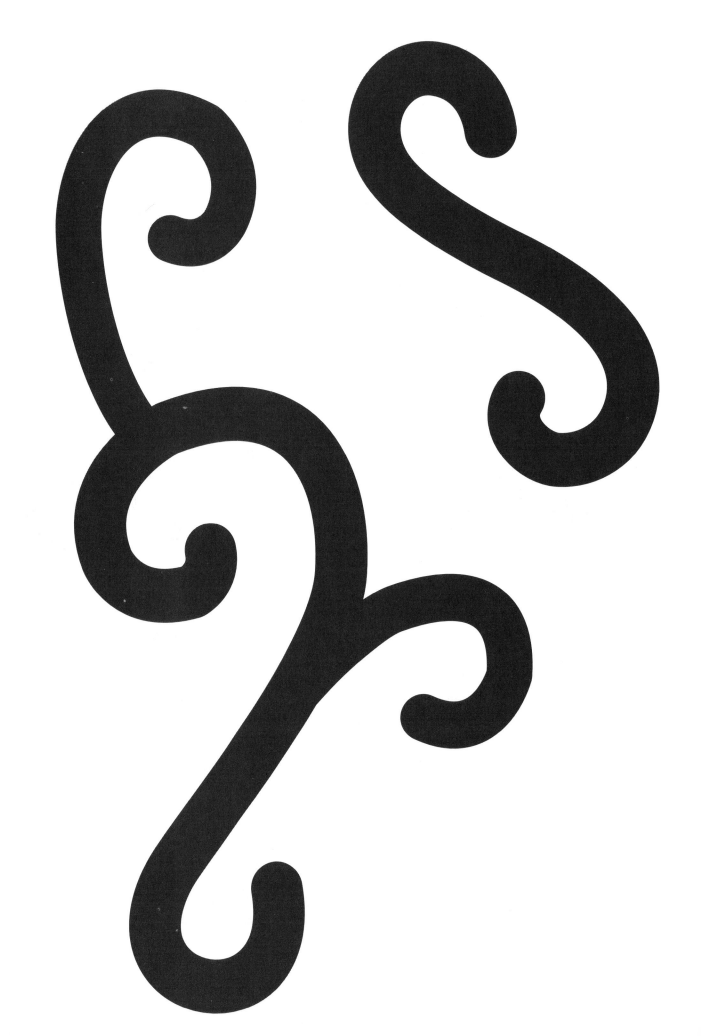

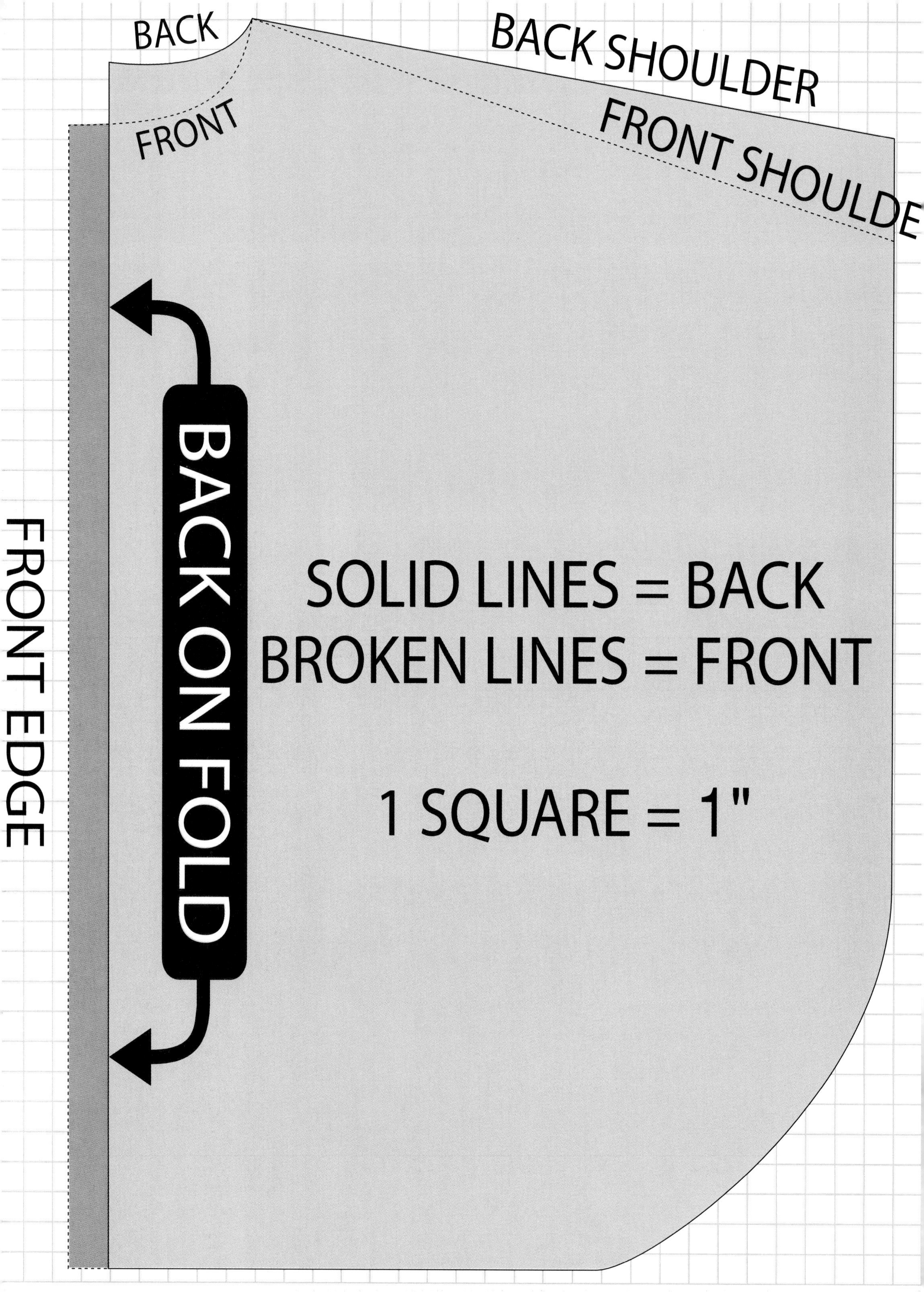

BACK

BACK SHOULDER

FRONT SHOULDE

FRONT

FRONT EDGE

BACK ON FOLD

SOLID LINES = BACK
BROKEN LINES = FRONT

1 SQUARE = 1"

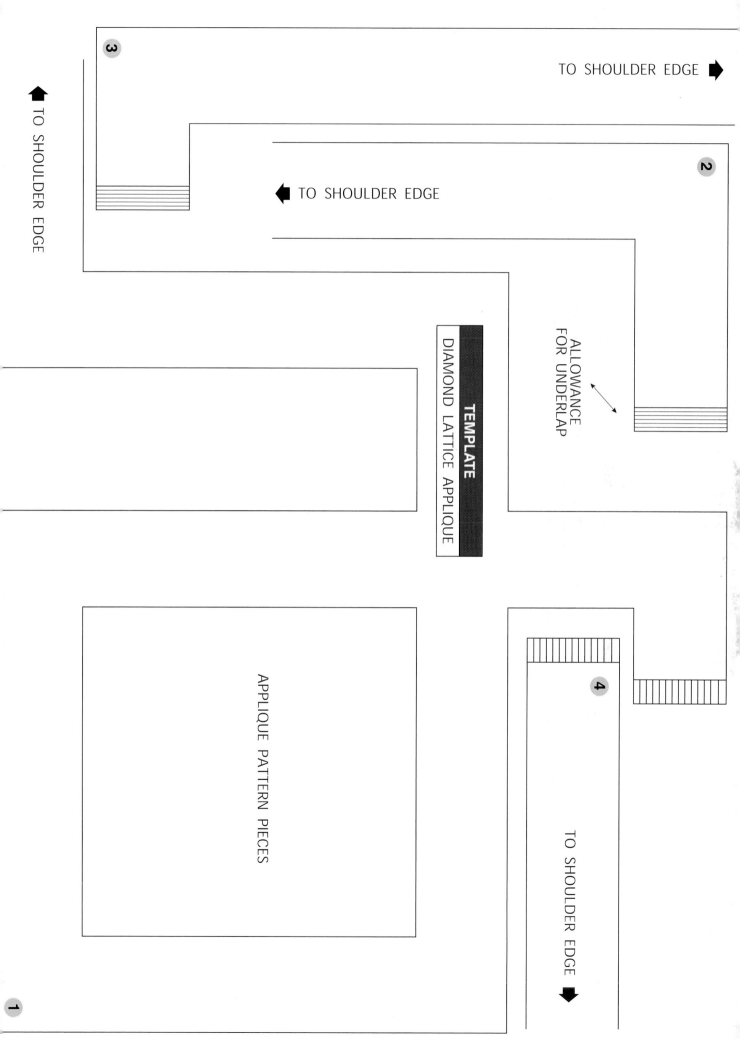

TO SHOULDER EDGE ➤

3

TO SHOULDER EDGE ▲

2

TO SHOULDER EDGE ◀

ALLOWANCE
FOR UNDERLAP

TEMPLATE
DIAMOND LATTICE APPLIQUE

APPLIQUE PATTERN PIECES

4

TO SHOULDER EDGE ▼

1

5 MINUTE HAT

USE ¼" SEAM ALLOWANCE

FABRIC: CUT 4 PIECES FROM POLAR FLEECE

RIBBING:

        ADULT: CUT 5" X 18" (OR CUT TO FIT)
        CHILD: CUT 5" X 16" (OR CUT TO FIT)

BAND:

        ADULT: CUT 20" SELF FABRIC BAND
        CHILD: CUT 18" SELF FABRIC BAND

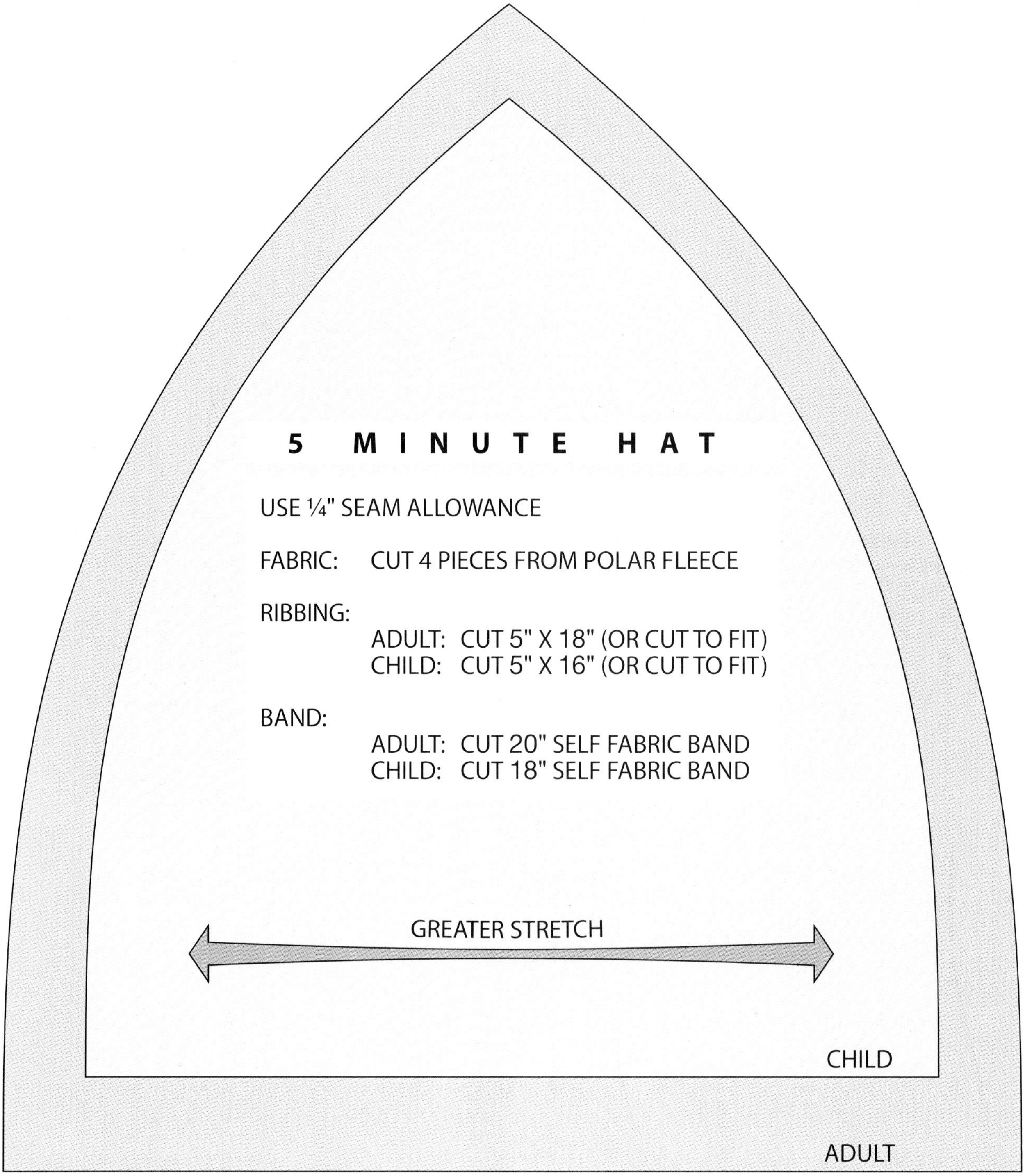

GREATER STRETCH

CHILD

ADULT

Index

Adhesives 33-34
Applique 109
Baby Applique 147
Baby Collection 146-147
Backwards Topstitching 65-66
Backwards Zipper 79-82
Blanket
    Baby Collection 146
    Baby Snuggle Wrap 148
    No Brainer 142
    Snuggle Bag 141-142
Blanket Stitch, Serger 143
Blunt-Edge Finish 49-50, 71-72, 83
Bottom Edge Finish (See Edge Finish)
Buttonholes
    Problems & Solutions 85-87
    Alternatives 87-89
Cape 137-139
Casings, elastic, elimination of 43
"Cheater's way" (See Edge Finishes)
Collars
    Blunt Edge Finish 50
    Copy Cat Designer Collar 41-42
    No-Fail Collar Change 42
Color Blocking 38-40
Cuffs (See Edge Finishes)
Cutting Fleece 27
Diamond Lattice Applique Pullover 135-136
Edge Finishes
    Elastic, Narrow 66-67
    Elastic, Wide 67
    Lycra Wrapped "Cheater's Way" 57-59
    Lycra Wrapped "Hard Way" 54-56
    Planning 53-54, 62-64
    Ribbing 59, 64
    Ribbing with Elastic 59-60, 64
    Self-Fabric, Fat Piping 60-65
Elastic
    Narrow, Cuffs and Bottom 66-67
    Stabilizing Shoulder Seam 48
    Wide, Cuffs and Bottom 67
    With Ribbing 59-60, 64
Embroidery 108-109
Fat Piping 60-64

Fleece Fabrics
    Brand Names, Mills, & Manufacturers 15-20
    Characteristics 20-23
Flower Pin 152
Fringe, Quick Technique 142-143
Hat
    5-Minute 145-146, 150-151
    6-Minute 151
Interfacing Buttonholes 87
Jacket, with dramatic sculpturing 132-134
Kilt, Little Lady's 145
Laundering 28
Lycra
    Trim Strips 52-54
    Wrapped Edges (See Edge Finishes)
Mittens, Quick Children's 151
Motifs, Sculpturing 104-106
Naptime Buddy 143-144
Needle Choices 29
No Side-Seam Techniques 44, 63-64
Notions, Specialty 32-33
Pattern Considerations 37-38
Pattern Layout & Cutting 27
Patchwork Pullover 139-141
Patchwork Yardage 140-141, 150
Pile Fabrics 20-23
Pintucks 106-107
Piping
    Fat Piping 60-64
    UltraSuede 96-97
Pockets
    Backwards, Patch 83
    Blunt Edge, Patch 49, 83
Pressing 28
Pretreating 28
Quilted-look Sculpturing 104
Ribbing
    Wimpy, Solution 64
    With Elastic 64
Right and Wrong Side Determination 25-26
Scarf
    Little Lady's 146
    Simple 151
Sculpturing
    Basics 99-102
    Check and Plaids 103
    Jacket With Dramatic Sculptured Back 132-134

Meandering 102-103
Motifs 104-106
Outline Quilted Look 104
Over-Sized Motifs 105-106
Seams
    5/8" Seam Options 47
    1/4" Seam Allowance 48
    Blunt Edge 49-50
    Lapped 48-49
    Stabilizing Shoulders Seam 48
Self Fabric Finish
    Bottom Band 65
    Cuffs 65
    Fat Piping 60-64
Serger Machine Basics 28-29
Sewing Machine Basics 28-29
Side Seam, Elimination 44
Snuggle Bag 141-142
Snuggle Baby Wrap 148
Sport Snaps 88-89
Stay, Pocket with Zipper 74-77
Troubleshooting 34-35
UltraSuede
    Buttonhole Loops 92
    Buttonhole Patches 93
    Buttonhole Patches with Loops 93
    Buttonhole Tabs 92
    Drawcord 91
    Hood Tie 91
    Piping 96-97
    Pocket Flaps 95-96
    Zippered Pockets 94
    Zipper Pulls 94-95
    Zipper Tab 95
    Yokes 96
Vest
    Little Lady's 146
    Make It Your Way 137
    No Side Seam 44, 63-64
Wrapped Edge Finishes (See Edge Finishes)
Zippered Pockets 74-78
Zippers
    "Dressed" 72-73
    "Naked" 72
    Backwards Zipper 79-82
    Blunt Edge 71-72
    Easy Zippered Pockets 74-77
    Insertion 71, 73
    Shortening 69-71
    Traditional 71
    Two-From-One Trick 77-78

ABOUT THE AUTHOR

Nancy Cornwell has been an avid sewer and designer for over thirty years. For the past sixteen years, she and her husband Jeff, have owned and operated **Stretch & Sew Fabrics/Bernina**, a retail fabric center in Lynnwood, Washington, where the focus is on better casual and sportswear fabrics.

Nancy's passion is in the design area. Each month she instructs her "I Love To Sew Club™" on how to take commercial patterns, cut them apart and re-design them to use as a base for reproducing ready-to-wear or creating new designs. She also shares these ideas, to a growing "by-mail" membership, by sending them across the United States and Canada.

Nancy is not a stranger to writing and publishing having previously authored two books: *The Best of I Love To Sew Club and Encore! More of The Best of I Love To Sew Club*. Each publication is a compilation of some of the most popular ideas presented in her club. In addition, she writes and publishes the nationally acclaimed *#1 Source* newsletter; a sewing newsletter that is published twice a month and mailed to subscribers across United States, Canada, Europe and Japan. The *#1 Source* newsletter keeps sewers up to date on the newest patterns, fabrics, notions, techniques and industry trends.

An accomplished speaker and guest lecturer, Nancy gives presentations to consumer groups, sewing shows and industry business conventions. For thirteen years she has been a featured speaker at the

Sewing & Stitchery Expo, sponsored by Washington State University Cooperative Extension, the largest home sewing consumer exposition in the country.

In answer to sewers' increasing demands for and difficulty in finding better fabrics, Nancy developed a national mail order service that services sewers across the nation. Geared for the discriminating sewer, she and her staff provide high quality coordinate knits, Polarfleece and all its "relatives," ready-to-wear overrun fabrics and the newest sewing information via the *#1 Source* newsletter.

For information on Nancy's **Stretch & Sew** national mail order service write:

Stretch & Sew Fabrics
Dept. AP
19725 40th Avenue W. #G
Lynnwood, WA 98036
mail order line: 425-776-3700
fax: 425-776-3551